The Suburbs of Heaven
The Diary of Murdoch Campbell

Thou wilt show me the path of life: in thy presence is fullness of joy; at thy right hand are pleasures for evermore.

Psalm 16: 11

The Suburbs of Heaven
The Diary of Murdoch Campbell

Edited by David Campbell

Covenanters Press

Covenanters Press
an imprint of
Zeticula Ltd
The Roan,
Kilkerran,
KA19 8LS,
Scotland.

http://www.covenanters.co.uk
admin@covenanters.co.uk

First published 2014

Text © David Campbell 2014

Front Cover: *Easter Ross Farms, looking towards the
Black Isle* © Donald M. Shearer 2014

Back Cover: *The Red Chair* © Janetta S. Gillespie 2014

ISBN 978-1-905022-33-5

In honour of

Mary Ann Campbell, née Fraser

1899 - 1991

With greatest affection and esteem

In memoriam

Donald M. MacKinnon

(1913 – 1994)

Acknowledgements

My warmest thanks to all who encouraged the publication of this Diary.

Particular thanks to my wife Evie for her practical help and considerable patience.

For comments on earlier drafts, thanks to Stephen Bostock, Donald MacLeod, John A. Morrison, and especially William E. Lyons.

Special thanks to Derek Prescott for skilled photographic work.

The painting *Easter Ross Farms, looking towards the Black Isle* by Donald M. Shearer is reproduced on the front cover with his kind permission, and the painting *The Red Chair* by Janetta S. Gillespie on the back cover © her estate.

DC

Preface

Some readers may have come across books written by my late father, the Revd Murdoch ('Murdo') Campbell, M.A., such as *Gleanings of Highland Harvest, The Loveliest Story Ever Told, Memories of a Wayfaring Man*, and *Wells of Joy*. His Foreword to this diary indicates that he would have welcomed its publication. It is of interest not only for his life and times, but also as one of the few documented accounts of 20th C Christian mysticism, extending across forty-one years. Its value is not only historical or academic, however. Such a record of fellowship with God is for many readers beyond price.

In our time interest in the topic of religious experience grew once William James had published *The Varieties of Religious Experience* (London: Longmans Green and Co. 1902). Like him, however, relatively few writers discuss the Biblical mysticism of Evangelical Protestants such as my father. *What* my father thought is clear: he believed he was on intimate terms with God. Here the Diary speaks for itself. But *how* he thought of this relation must sometimes be drawn out from between the lines. Tentatively, both in this *Preface* and in a few footnotes, I discuss briefly his mysticism and its relation to matters such as knowledge, faith, and altruism. My aim throughout is to be sympathetic but not to take sides.

Religious mysticism is sometimes confused with poetic feeling, magic tricks, dark powers, even lunacy. Because it is reclusive and mysterious, some mystics despair of finding a sympathetic ear and withdraw as it were to a hermitage. In writing about their interior life they also withdraw from ordinary declarative language, feeling that it is inadequate to describe their mystical experience. Indeed the mere attempt to articulate the ineffable involves 'practical contradiction'. They resort instead to figurative language, such as metaphor and simile; thus a mystic might without embarrassment speak of God as a rock or light. Perhaps religious language is never plain prose (unlike related historical language, for example).

My father had the independence of mind, confidence, and courage not merely to keep a diary of his interior religious life but also to prepare it for publication. The resulting diary, level-headed and perceptive, reveals him as not in any way credulous, but as adept at detecting deceit and delusion. Nevertheless while recording without apology what he believed was a gift of intimate fellowship with God, his diary reveals that he was a warm-hearted and humorous human being.

Indeed to observe my father, as I did over many years, you could scarcely doubt this avowal of a gift of divine fellowship. But such an observation is, of course, second-hand evidence. First-hand mystical experience may dispel all doubt for the mystic but it cannot do so for others. Corroboration by even a fellow mystic is impossible since mystical experiences are the experience of only one person, the subject of them, and are admittedly indescribable in ordinary descriptive language.

For my father, it seems that there could be no greater pleasure than daily converse with God. This pleasure is distributed unequally among people, not like a cake, of which you have less if I have more, but rather in the sense that some people have perfect pitch but most of us do not. And no particular pattern of experience is required of a believer.

Reading the diary confronts us with the question about whether a self-forgetting regard for others, or altruism, is the greatest good even if it brings us little of what people might think of as pleasure or satisfaction. This question also reminds us that Jesus taught that we should have great concern for the poor, even when that concern's only reward might be suffering. The diary also clearly assumes that faith is not simply a matter of rote dogma but involves a personal relation to God, and that the Gospel speaks to individual souls in the quiet hour as well as promulgates a social and ethical message for all. For while Jesus said, "you have the poor always with you" (*Mat.* 26: 11) and intimated that they must be attended to, he also said that, in her quiet reticence, "Mary has chosen [the] good part". (*Luke* 10: 40-42) For God waits graciously to communicate with each of us individually, calling on us to confess our sins, act justly and show mercy, if only we might listen. The mystic, the diary reveals, is the one who listens and hears God more than do others.

The Diary also reveals that he was clairvoyant, and gives many examples. The *Biographical Notes* looks at some of these and at their implications. He was intrigued, though idly: his interest lay in Christianity, not psychic research. He took the line that a clairvoyant experience is spiritually inconsequent unless backed by a specific passage of Scripture.

Many Diary entries record that some spiritual problem or other of his was resolved, but he says little about the circumstances. Generally speaking, as a spiritual record, the diary does not trade in ordinary incidents and idiosyncrasies. Instead, in recording the mystic's privileged closeness to God, it aims to deflect us from the world and its daily chatter and its material things to a direct communion with God. Just as to the lover, the revelation of the beloved's attitudes and feelings towards him or her means so much more than knowledge of any material gifts or dowry.

Since it records significant interior moments in a deeply religious life, the diary is organised by dates, but not as a narrative with a beginning, middle and end. However, some of my footnotes include background information, and in both the Diary and the *Biographical Notes* I quote from *Memories of a Wayfaring Man*, since this memoir overlaps chronologically at some points with the diary and so deepens our understanding of what he records.

Finally, in both the *Diary* and *Biographical Notes*, I retain my father's sub-Jacobean style of writing as normal in his day, and follow him also in writing 'His' with a capital letter for God in possessive mode, except within quotations, where it follows the King James Bible in using lower case.

David Campbell
Strachur, Argyll

Contents

Illustrations

The Revd Murdoch Campbell, 1957

Foreword

Should other eyes than mine see this personal diary, I should like to say that my only and real reason for its existence is that I might, with regard to time and circumstances, exactly record those events which, I hope, stand related to my spiritual life. With the sun of my pilgrimage now in decline I might soon fail to recall some things which I have mentioned, and which I cannot but prize. For many years now what I most value is the repeated experience of God, as I sincerely believe it is, bestowing on me His comfort, guidance and grace through His Word. This He has done on many occasions not only during waking hours but also 'in the night watches'.[1] This converse with God through His Word has produced an indelible conviction in my mind that He is intimately and personally present with His people in this world and that His care for them, in both His grace and providence, is inconceivably tender and all-embracing. For this reason only, I would not object to the diary being printed. To Him be the glory.

Murdoch Campbell
Inverness 1971

---

1 'The somewhat "mystic" vein which runs through my story I thought of suppressing, but on second thoughts I decided to let it stand. This I did because it is, as I hope, something wholly related to the inspired Word of God.' (*Memories of a Wayfaring Man* [M], Introduction) Murdo Campbell points out that his mysticism was far from unique, as is confirmed by acquaintances and Christian biography. (M 55) One consequence is that mysticism is not an aberration, either individual or collective.

Dazzled, circa 1930

1930

August 20, 1930

On this lovely summer day I was inducted as minister to my first charge, at Fort Augustus and Glenmoriston in Inverness-shire.[2] The 'laying on of hands' was solemnly carried out. I pray that the Minister of the true sanctuary would also place His hand on my head. I am full of unfamiliar feelings, and I cannot help anticipating the future. May the Lord prevent me from bringing dishonour on His glorious name and cause.

November 27, 1930

This day I married the 'only' girl.[3] I felt the Lord had provided her for me. May the dear Lord keep us, and unite us in His own sweet love both in time and throughout Eternity. My wife is dispositionally calm and composed, a thing which I cannot always say of myself.

---

2   This charge was bilingual in the sense that the Glenmoriston part was Gaelic and Fort Augustus English. At that time the charge was a considerable size.

3   Mary ('Molly') Fraser came from Strathpeffer in Ross-shire, then a fashionable spa, where she opened a bookshop. Her family hailed from Glenurquhart in Inverness-shire.

1931

February 6, 1931

This morning about 4.00 a.m. I woke myself up calling to my dear mother[4], whom I saw, in a dream, ascending as in a bright mist to the sky. The vision awed my spirit; that was what caused me to call out, "Mother!" After this, in the morning, word came that she had passed away at that very time, 4.00 a.m. And so the dearest bond in life, except one, has been dissolved. How can I repay her love and devotion to me? But I am happy in the hope that she is now in Heaven.

February 9, 1931

This day we buried dear Mother's remains near the spot where she was born. And the subdued murmur of the tireless ocean will go on until the last trump shall sound and the dead in Christ arise. My native island of Lewis feels empty now, and our hearth has lost its most attractive ornament. "When my father and my mother forsake me, then the Lord will take me up." (*Psalms* 27:10)

---

4   Murdo Campbell's mother was Christiana Campbell, née MacLean, from Swainbost.

1932

April 4, 1932

This morning my beloved wife gave birth to a boy who appears to be unwell. Her own condition is normal, for which I praise the Most High. Stayed all day with our darling boy, and felt I could give my life for his.

April 5, 1932

At 8.10 this morning our dear child passed into the eternal world. I felt all comfort and joy had fled away for ever. I shall go to him, but he cannot come to me.

Later I deposited his little frame into the cold grave at Fort Augustus. My darling's arms are empty, and our hearts are pierced through with sorrow.[5]

---

5 'A few years after this bereavement... I walked up a quiet hillside road from which I thought I could see far across Loch Ness toward the place where our child's body lay...a voice seemed to speak out of the stillness: "In my Father's House are many mansions". ...I then knew it was well with the child and that by God's grace I would see him again in the Place where tears are unknown.' (M 45)

Glenmoriston Free Church and Manse, circa 2000

1933

March 10, 1933

This is a night to be remembered. Before the evening service I enjoyed a sweet hour of communion with my Lord.[6] I had a distinct view of Eternity, and of the preciousness of the Gospel. I felt myself an immortal soul, and in saving touch with God. I preached on a theme which appeals to my heart: human inability, and the power and sufficiency of Christ.

July 17, 1933

Last night in my sleep I heard a song which has affected my soul ever since. It was the last verse of Psalm 16, sung in Gaelic: "Thou wilt show me the path of life: in thy presence is fullness of joy; at thy right hand there are pleasures for evermore". The singing, in its beauty and melody, excelled all I ever heard. It was like something from a holier and fairer world. My soul is still warm and amazed. May I spend Eternity in such a frame of mind.[7]

---

6   For Murdo Campbell, communion does not mean union. Some suppose that a mystic loses himself in God, like a drop in the ocean. One problem is that he cannot then be identified as an individual, who could be party to a relationship; there can be no relationship. Similarly you speak of the 'object' of love to distinguish you from the beloved. Presumably, also, you could not otherwise engage in dialogue.

7   'It was in Fort Augustus that I had one of my first vivid experiences of God, by His Word, comforting me in "the night watches". ...These words also came wrapped in music such as I seldom heard in this world. This staff of comfort the Lord graciously placed, as it were, in my hand as I was entering upon my life's work.' (M 43-44)

1934

May 21, 1934

The congregation of Partick Highland, Glasgow, are sending me a Call.[8] If I leave the dear people here [in Glenmoriston and Fort Augustus], I shall carry with me pleasant memories of my first ecclesiastical love. Here I was happy, not least in my home life, and the people have shown me much love.

June 6, 1934

I accepted the Call to Glasgow. A decision whose propriety only the future can reveal. May the Lord make the path clear before me. I go, like Abraham, "not knowing whither". (*Hebrews* 11: 8) Let me have his faith in my God.

June 11, 1934

At a Communion in Strontian, Argyll.[9] On Saturday evening on the way to Church I had an almost overwhelming sense of the Lord's Presence. "It is the Lord." (*John* 21: 7) Now "I know that my redeemer liveth" and that He is mine, and I am His. (*Job* 19: 25) This hour was worth a thousand worlds to my poor soul.

The couple I am lodging with love the Lord, and the atmosphere in their home is sweetened by His presence.

---

8   'I had been called to the young – and at that time somewhat disturbed – congregation of Partick Highland Church.' (M 47)
9   A 'Communion' is the celebration of the sacrament of the Lord's Supper, normally twice a year, by each congregation in Murdo Campbell's denomination. Guest preachers conduct five or more services from the Thursday 'Fast Day' to the Monday 'Thanksgiving'. The Communion service is held on Sunday, the Sabbath, when communicants share bread and wine at 'the Lord's Table'.

I have much travelling, to Communions.

My wife took ill, but words in Psalm 128 assured me that she would recover.[10]

September 6, 1934

This evening I was solemnly inducted to the pastoral charge of Partick Highland Free Church. Attempted to utter a few words of thanks for gifts received. Rather troubled at my presumption in coming to this great city. Yet if the Lord has called me here I must not so trouble myself.

---

10 'In some real way I felt urged, as by another voice, to open the Book and read. The words on which my eyes rested were those of Psalm 128: "Blessed is every one that feareth the Lord ...happy shalt thou be, and it shall be well with thee...Yea, thou shalt see thy children's children, and peace upon Israel." ...I felt like one on the fringe of a world of infinite blessedness. A sense of indescribable consolation filled my heart ...I then told my wife that all would be well and that her life was to be prolonged and preserved.' (M 48)

1935

January 7, 1935

Concludes a week of prayers. Well attended, and the atmosphere warm. I have difficulty in determining whether those who manifest emotion are all genuine. The natural feelings may be affected by the Truth, as in the Lord's parable of the Sower. Emotion without discernment, and feeling without holiness, are of no worth. I must beware of those who show feeling, but whose lives are at fault.

One night, in Strachur, Argyll, as a weight of sin and its sorrow sensibly pressed upon my spirit, I retired to my bedroom to pray. I was given a wonderful sense of deliverance and peace. [11]

---

11 'Standing before an open window, through which streamed the warm air of the summer evening, my whole inward being came instantly under this reviving light and heavenly love. For two weeks afterwards I walked in the light of Christ's face ...there was a depth and a constancy in this enjoyment which surpassed anything I had hitherto experienced. ...I climbed solitary hills and took quiet walks where I could escape the presence of men... In that beloved Argyllshire village I dwelt for a season in the suburbs of Heaven.' (M 49-50)

1937

June 1937

On holiday at Prestwick, Ayrshire with my wife, and daughter Anne. Never again would I come to a place like this in the summer time. The crowds are oppressive.

September 21, 1937

This morning my wife was delivered of a second baby girl, to be called Mary Fraser, after herself. Both are well. I hope that I am not guilty of presumption in believing that our child, like her sister Anne, is in the "everlasting covenant, ordered in all things and sure". (2 *Samuel* 23: 5) The Lord bless her and make her a star to shine on His side in this world.

On holiday

1939

June 8, 1939

My dear father is with us in Glasgow for a holiday. His 'company and story' are much relished. He preached for me on several occasions. His contact with a better and older generation has made his life more gracious than we are now accustomed to. [12]

September 3, 1939

At a Communion in the island of Coll. The people were somewhat distracted during the 'action' sermon. No wonder: they knew, as I did not, that Britain had just declared war on Germany. What sorrow and changes will this war bring? We trust in God. [13]

A strange dream I had recently about Hitler has filled me with a sense of mystery. I dreamt that in the hour of twilight I was alone in a wide field standing before a big loom, which was in motion by some invisible means. From its front there projected two shelves, on each of which lay a book. With the vibration of the loom the nearer shelf not only shook but gradually rose. The

12 'In 1947 we visited my father in Skye. For fourteen years he had laboured in Waternish... He was entering upon the last mile... One day as we sat with [him] in his lodgings, one of our children came in. I quietly reminded him of the way his own mother had left her blessing to me and suggested that he, if the Lord so moved him, should bless our child also. Without another word they walked into another room where he prayed earnestly beside the child.' (M 77)
    The last time we saw him 'his mind and memory had now no grasp whatever of anything related to this life [but] he could still sing his favourite psalms, and pray without misquoting a word of Scripture.' (M 78)
    Alexander Campbell's minister in Ness, the Revd Duncan MacDougall, wrote to Murdo Campbell: 'Although we had a godly Kirk Session, every man of them outstanding, yet I might truly say that your father was a man by himself'. (M 79)
13 In the autumn of 1939 'a thousand young men [mobilised in Lewis]... crowded into the waiting ship... A great silence fell on the crowd. ...A lone melodious voice began to sing verses from the forty-sixth Psalm: "God is our refuge and our strength..." The huge crowd took up the words... This was not a display of feeling, but an expression of that trust in God which dwelt in many hearts.' (M 9-10)

book resting on this shelf was an old volume bound in yellow calf, which I felt intuitively was a good book, either the Bible, or some work of piety. On the farther shelf there lay another book, whose title was *Mein Kampf*, by Adolf Hitler. This shelf also vibrated, but unlike the other, it did not rise. After a while I saw a man place a wedge below the shelf on which his book rested, and give it several terrific blows. I waited for the whole thing to break in pieces. His idea was to make his book rise above the other; but he failed. After he had struck the blows, a change came over his face; and, as if some hidden power had smitten him, the hammer and wedge fell from his hands, and he rolled back with the cry, 'When I come to die!' Then he lay dead in front of the great loom, which continued as if it had not been touched.

This vision made a great impression on my mind; I can still see it as if it were last night. My interpretation of it is that Hitler is going to lose the war and die in the very act of trying to impose his system on the world; and that no man can impose his will on God's. Providence cannot be frustrated. However dark the hour for Britain she will not be conquered. But, as no man must place any trust in these visions of the night, I afterwards sought God's Word in the matter, and while earnestly praying for this, a portion of Scripture came powerfully before my mind: *Ps.* 136: 23, 24. "Who remembered us in our low estate: for his mercy endureth forever: And hath redeemed us from our enemies: for his mercy endureth forever." Fortified in my soul by it, I intimated to my people my strong persuasion that God would give us deliverance at last. But He alone knows what sufferings we shall have to pass through before then.[14]

14 '...some would object to any reliance even on Scripture as unsafe and foolish unless it is conveyed to us during our conscious hours when the mind is normal and capable of rational activity... [But] was not Jacob nearer to God in his Bethel dream than at any other time in his life? ...Christian biography in every age gives innumerable instances of such communications. ...And this converse with God in Christ is an invaluable apologetic which doubt and atheism can never gainsay. It is also something which they can never understand nor believe.' (M 52-56)

1940

August 16, 1940

Home after spending some weeks in Plymouth and Portsmouth. Very exhausted, having had few nights undisturbed by the sounding of those horrible sirens. Their wail has everything in it suggestive of death, woe and untold sorrow. These often come with them. I noticed that whenever they sound, birds and animals seem to cease to sing or behave normally. They instinctively realise approaching danger. Two bombs fell on the Barracks at Portsmouth, and some of us escaped death by yards. A great shock to one's system. Enjoyed preaching to these dear boys, and was sorry to leave them. The Germans are apparently going to bomb 'military objectives' in the very heart of our big towns. Lord, prepare us for this cup of woe.[15]

15 'In Portsmouth I had my first experience of a severe air-raid, on the naval barracks there. On a cloudless day...a warning was sounded...huge quantities of mud and debris poured over us...' (M 61)

1941

January 23, 1941

Our poor country is bleeding under the fierce onslaught of the German bombers. Yet I am so seldom on my knees while this calamity is passing. Much comforted by the last verses of the 68th Psalm: "Ascribe ye strength unto God: his excellency is over Israel, and his strength is in the clouds. O God, thou art terrible out of thy holy places: the God of Israel is he that giveth strength and power unto his people. Blessed be God."

March 15, 1941

Severe air raids on Glasgow, especially on the Clydebank area.[16] One night about this time we slept beneath a stair, for doubtful protection. As I awoke the words were present with me, "Wait on the Lord and keep his way, and he shall exalt thee to inherit the land: when the wicked are cut off, thou shalt see it". (*Ps.* 37: 34)[17]

April 21, 1941

Took upon myself to write Mr Winston Churchill a letter of encouragement. I told him of my strong conviction that Germany was to lose the war. I enclosed a note to his private secretary to be sure to refer my note to his chief. He did so, for I had an acknowledgement a few days ago in which Mr Churchill

---

16 'It was on a clear and lovely night in 1941 that the German bombers made a devastating attack on Clydeside. ...That night the moon was full, the weather mild, and the stars, so bright and peaceful, seemed unusually near and kindly... Our boy [of eighteen months] had an idea that all the noise outside was created for his own special entertainment! With the crash of each distant bomb he would look up and smile... he had entered a cruel and fallen world but as yet he knew it not. (M 61-62)

17 'Never "in the night watches" did I find the Word of the Lord in my mouth but in answer to prayer, and as the arrow of the Lord's deliverance in some trial, or of exhortation or encouragement in some duty.' (M 54)

conveyed his thanks. I also wrote the *Glasgow Herald* an answer to General Franco, who advises the British to give in as they must lose the war. One reader called me 'a presumptuous prophet', as he himself strongly believes in Britain's downfall. But I have not spoken out of my own head, nor given my own dream: I have the mind of the Lord, I hope, in this matter. If not, I shall be a miserable man.

April 28, 1941

Family evacuated to Glenmoriston; I stay on in Glasgow.[18]

September 12, 1941

For the last few nights I had a most blessed experience. I was greatly helped and urged in my soul to wrestle with God for His Cause in the world. In this duty I was greatly aided, I trust, by the Holy Spirit. My only plea was that the everlasting arm of Jehovah might be exerted to deliver His Cause, now menaced from so many sides. I got the impression in my soul that already His arm was raised, but first to destroy and demolish those systems of iniquity which had challenged His authority. Babylon must be laid low ere Zion be raised up in glory. Oh, my soul, rejoice in thy God, and thank Him for this season of fellowship with Him.

---

18 'The following week I moved the family to our beloved Glenmoriston while I remained with my flock in Glasgow...One early morning ...I suddenly collapsed through overwork.' (M 67) Murdo Campbell's pastoral workload remained excessive until he moved to Resolis, in the Black Isle, in 1951.

1953

It is now a long time since I made any entries in this Diary. Continuing physical exhaustion during the difficult years of the war and its aftermath demanded a change from the incessant activities of a large city charge.[19] I am now settled in Resolis, in the Black Isle, where I hope my health may improve. May the Lord bless my work here, and restore my strength in some measure. This is a quiet pastoral corner of our Highlands, and we do enjoy the loveliness of the countryside.[20]

November 17, 1953

In Edinburgh for meetings of Church committees. A ministerial friend was with me at the hotel; I had no previous knowledge of his Christian life and experience. In the early morning I awoke with the words, "...my goodness extended not to thee; but to the saints that are in the earth, and to the excellent, in whom is all my delight". (*Ps.* 16: 2, 3) In these words the Lord assured me, I believe, that we were bound in the love of Christ, and to others of the brethren whom I was to meet this day.

December 12, 1953

Had a dream that I was in view of Scalpay isle in Harris. A calm sea dazzled in the bright light of a summer sun. It was a lovely scene. I awoke soon afterwards with the words, "Yea, the sparrow hath found an house, and the swallow a nest for herself...". (*Ps.* 84: 3) It appears that "the Lord is there" (*Ezekiel* 48: 35), and that He is preparing this now vacant charge for a pastor.

19 Murdo Campbell does not say why he discontinued the Diary between 1941 and 1953. However, the exhaustion he refers to would seem to have been reason enough.

20 The Black Isle peninsula lies on the arable eastern fringe of the Scottish mountains. '[O]ne could not but observe that where the Lord had once reaped a great harvest the land was now almost spiritually barren... The moral tone of the community, however, remained on a high level.' (M 100)

December 21, 1953

Visited a lady in the Creagan, Resolis who referred feelingly to my sermon on the words, "...and my delights were with the sons of men". (*Proverbs* 8: 31) Before preaching it I had prayed that the Lord would lead me to someone who needed "a word in season". (*Isaiah* 50: 4)

December 22, 1953

Before six o'clock this morning the Lord again gave me the promise and blessing of Psalm 32: 1: "Blessed is he whose transgression is forgiven, whose sin is covered". On the lap of this word I slept again for about an hour. I then awoke in a state of great comfort with the words of Isaiah, 54: 9, 10 articulate within my spirit.[21] These precious promises, like pearls from the deep sea of God's eternal love, I treasured in my heart. Afterwards I reminded myself on my knees before the Lord that although His anger is passed away from His people, He still brings chastisement upon them for their sin. May I therefore rejoice with trembling.

---

21 "For this is as the waters of Noah unto me: for as I have sworn that the waters of Noah should no more go over the earth; so have I sworn that I would not be wroth with thee, nor rebuke thee. For the mountains shall depart, and the hills be removed; but my kindness shall not depart from thee, neither shall the covenant of my peace be removed, saith the Lord that hath mercy on thee."

December 28, 1953

I was disturbed all day because of the words, "Come, behold the works of the Lord, what desolations he hath made in the earth". (*Ps.* 46: 8) This verse fastened itself on my mind, and I had a distinct and distressing impression that God would again permit the desolation of the land, if not of the world, in war.

Read *John* 12, and a chapter from the life of David Brainerd.

December 31, 1953

Walked to Newhall, Resolis, in the afternoon to see an old woman who is dying. I found her alone and asleep. Offered a brief but silent prayer. On the way home I thought of that great day when the grave shall give up its dead, and when those who sleep in Jesus shall arise in glory. I found much sweetness in the words:

"These eyes shall see Him in that day
The *God* that died for me,
And all my rising bones shall say
Lord, who is like to Thee?"

1954

January 1, 1954

Awake while the rest of the household were still asleep, and sought to commit myself and mine, my times and my destiny, into God's strong hand. I prayed for the revival and increase of Christ's Kingdom. Had a sweet communion and a feeling of sympathy with the great multitude on earth who pray continually for Christ in His Cause, and for the increase and extension of His Kingdom. "...let the whole earth be filled with his glory." (*Ps.* 72: 19) Just as there is a constant intercession going on "within the veil" (*Heb.* 6: 19) for the Church on earth, so there is a never-ceasing "pillar of smoke" (*Song of Solomon* 3: 6) going up to Heaven: the prayers of the Church for her Lord. This encouraged me greatly; for all these prayers shall yet be answered. I felt that the Lord smiled upon my soul and prayer, on this the first day of another year.

February 24, 1954

The last words of Psalm 27 came fresh from the lips of the Comforter: "Wait on the Lord: be of good courage, and he shall strengthen thine heart: wait, I say, on the Lord". [22] They contain the promise of the strength I greatly need and pray for.

March 26, 1954

Returned from Glasgow, where I introduced my successor in Partick. [23] While there I was greatly refreshed by the words of Paul, "Having, therefore, obtained help of God I continue unto this day..." (*Acts* 26: 22) Without God and His help, Paul would have perished in his many afflictions.

22 The Diary in effect distinguishes *believing* that God forgives the repentant from *knowing* Him as Comforter and Confidant by personal, one-to-one acquaintance. Such contact with God is not schematic, and in this respect differs in kind from say, acceptance of the Scheme of Redemption.
23 Murdo Campbell's successor in Partick Highland Free Church was the Revd Malcolm Morrison.

This morning I was comforted by the words: "... my soul ... hope thou in God: for I shall yet praise him". (*Ps.* 42: 11)

April 10, 1954

Had a letter from Canada giving the time and circumstances of Uncle Alex's death.[24] The lady who wrote believed he died in the Lord. The previous day, before I heard of his death, I was much affected by the words, "Precious in the sight of the Lord is the death of his saints". (*Ps.* 116: 15) Heard also with much sorrow of the departure of a certain minister who was a good man, and of unusual intellectual powers.

April 17, 1954

I had occasion to offer a rebuke, which I did, but not in the spirit of charity. Afterwards I was in great sorrow of heart. "For the wrath of man worketh not the righteousness of God." (*James* 1: 20) Love alone never fails. Behind all these stumblings and ensnarings I can discern the wiles of the adversary. But before dawn today, He who abundantly pardons visited my distressed spirit in the words: "for I shall yet praise him, who is the health of my countenance, and my God". (*Ps.* 42: 11) These precious words helped to sweeten the "waters of Marah". (*Exodus* 15: 23)

May 24, 1954

Returned from the Assembly meetings in Edinburgh. Had moments of communion with the Lord in His own Word, at my lodgings there. God brought me very near to a dear one in the words, "But the mercy of the Lord is from everlasting to everlasting upon them that fear him, and his righteousness unto children's children..." (*Ps.* 103: 17)

Dreamt that I was in my late father's company, and that together we sang the words of Psalm 34, v. 22:

24 Many of Murdo Campbell's relatives emigrated to the U.S.A. and Canada, losing touch with their families who remained in Lewis.

"The Lord redeems his servants' souls
None perish that him trust."

In Edinburgh I was also most powerfully affected by the words of Psalm 118, v. 16, "The right hand of the Lord is exalted; the right hand of the Lord doeth valiantly". The words quite drenched my whole spirit, melting me down, and filling me for the rest of the day with indescribable consolation.

August 16, 1954

Sitting in the Resolis study, with the rising sun throwing its soft light over the distant woods, and with the rest of the household still asleep, I found a precious experience. As I read again the Book of *Genesis* I was much affected by God's sovereign condescension and love in communing with man.[25] "The God of Abraham." (*Ex.* 3: 6) Had a strange and overpowering feeling of kinship with those dear men of old who walked with God. Though a poor halting sinner, I hope their God is my God; and this unbroken link with them seemed to eliminate time and space, and to bring us together in the One Person, the Redeeming Angel of the Covenant.

August 17, 1954

Awoke this morning much affected by the words of David, "Oh, that one would give me a drink of the water of the well of Bethlehem, which is by the gate!" (2 *Samuel* 23: 15) A fit description of my thirst for likeness to Christ, and conformity to His revealed Will. Oh, that my faith, love and hope might break through my spiritual bondage and, like David's mighty men, bring me a cool soul-refreshing drink from the Fountain of Life.

25 Murdo Campbell finds God's condescension in conversing with sinners 'amazing', or difficult to understand. In another way however this is *impossible* to understand, like saying for example that the dead will rise, that God is love despite suffering, that He rules despite chance, and so on. For some, understanding follows belief; yet one reason you need faith is that you can never understand.

August 31, 1954

For several days I had been enjoying much spiritual peace. My heart was warm and my mind composed. But for the last few days my skies have lowered. Satan, by a terrifying temptation, threw me into darkness and confusion; but the dear Redeemer, the Brother who was born for adversity, came seasonably to me in the words which were also His own prayer in His sufferings, "O Lord: O my strength, haste thee to help me". (*Ps.* 22: 19) With these words I endeavoured to resist the enemy. They also became my prayer to the One who alone can bruise his head. Derived much comfort from the words, "Hitherto hath the Lord helped us". (1 *Sam.* 7: 12) My Heavenly Friend has His caring eye on me.

September 16, 1954

Rev A. MacLeod, the Free Church minister at Back, in the island of Lewis, is dying. A strong man physically, he refused to slow his pace with the coming on of the years. He knew the Lord and served Him with zeal. I used to envy his strength; but here I am, still spared, and the stronger man fallen.

September 23, 1954

Had news this week of the departure to his everlasting rest of a dear friend whose recollection of his former sins, his constant sense of a heart "desperately wicked", (*Jeremiah* 17: 9) and his fear of not being received "at the gate", (*Genesis* 23: 10) left him a humble, trembling man all his life. He went the whole way to Heaven with his head bowed. 'Mr Fearing' is now beyond all his fears. God dwelt with this good man.

September 24, 1954

Called on Mr MacLeod, the Back minister, in hospital. He clung to me affectionately as he related, in almost inaudible whispers, God's goodness to him in his illness. We embraced as we separated, to meet no more in time. Now he is gone to enjoy an unfading inheritance with Christ. After I had said 'Farewell', and had closed the door of his bedroom, I was constrained to go back and to quote the words of the Redeemer, "But I will see you again, and your heart shall rejoice, and your joy no man taketh from you". (*John* 16: 22) He waved me his last farewell. I am most happy that we thus parted in love and peace.

October 21, 1954

Was much disturbed last night over my constant lapses from the standard which the Lord sets before me in His Word. The Tables of the Law are so often broken in my hands; but they were not broken in the hands of my Substitute. In the night I was much helped by the words:

"As far as east is distant from
the west, so far hath he
From us removed in his love
all our iniquity." (*Ps.* 103: 12)

The more I thought about these words, the more their incomparable glory appeared to me. In them I saw anew the infinite magnitude of the love which constrained our great Redeemer to leave Heaven to become our Sin-bearer, appointed by God to carry our sin into the unknown and undiscoverable land of God's forgetfulness. If my sins are covered and put away by the blood of Christ then it is *impossible* that they and I should ever meet again.

October 28, 1954

The felt spiritual death among us in these parts often fills me with sorrow. This dark cloud overshadowed my spirit after I went to rest. In the early morning I awoke with the words, "To see thy power and thy glory, so as I have seen thee in the sanctuary ". (*Ps.* 63: 2) Will I get even a glimpse of the coming Millennial Day, as Moses saw the Land of Promise - from afar?

November 17, 1954

Have been looking again at one of my Scriptural jewels. It is now almost two years since the Lord met me in the words, "Casting all your care upon him, for he careth for you". (1 *Peter* 5: 7) Yesterday, after several vexatious experiences, these words returned to calm my heart. Their gracious and far-reaching implications demand great faith and grace if we are to rest in and believe their promise. I should not be "troubled about too many things" (*Luke* 10: 41) and know so little of the trustful heart that rests, in all circumstances, at Jesus' feet. This is my infirmity.

November 23, 1954

Had preached in a state of great bondage. I was tongue-tied, spirit-bound, and greatly embarrassed. But the Lord graciously relieved me on Saturday afternoon by drawing me very sweetly to Himself. I walked outdoors for nearly two hours in a state of calm assurance of God's love. I tried to take advantage of this favourable tide by sending forth many prayers which I hope may return, in their time, laden with blessings.

On Sabbath morning I felt very near in spirit to a certain Elder in Gairloch, Wester Ross. The words, "To this man will I look, even to him that is poor and of a contrite spirit and trembleth at my words", were present with me. (*Is.* 66: 2) But I do not know why he was so much in my thoughts at that hour.

December 4, 1954

In the last week one of my favourite 'texts', like a silver bell, awoke me out of sleep. "As the mountains are about Jerusalem, so is the Lord about his people from henceforth even for ever." (*Ps.* 125: 2) The deep discouragement I experienced on the previous days lifted somewhat, by means of these helpful and reassuring words. They teach me that my hope is good though often tried, and that the Lord is near though I do not always apprehend Him.

December 9, 1954

Yesterday after some spiritual conflict I went to pray. In my folly I asked the Lord to save me from some of my sufferings. As I was praying I had a feeling that this impatient and wrong request was a treacherous rock on which one could suffer damage.

After I went to rest a young man I did not know, whose lovely face bore the marks of much sorrow, stood before me in a dream and quoted the words, "For unto you it is given on behalf of Christ not only to believe in him, but also to suffer for his sake". (*Philippians* 1: 29) In this gracious but curious way the Holy One brought me back into the path of wisdom and resignation. The words cast a kind, composing light on the meaning and dignity of such suffering. It is the token of His love, and the pledge of Heaven.

December 14, 1954

Last night was much overcome by the Psalmist's prayer for grace to do the revealed will of the Lord, "Teach me to do thy will; for thou art my God". (*Ps.* 143: 10) It is not enough to know His will; we must also love it.

How utterly insignificant these personal remarks of mine are in the light of all the solemn events and potential terrors of this terrible age. The world seems to be rushing into the greatest storm it has yet encountered.

1955

January 3, 1955

On New Year's morning I was again able to leave myself and mine in God's faithful Hand, and under His watchful Eye. I prayed, not without tears, that He might take care of my family, and provide them, if that be His will, with helpmeets in their own spiritual image and likeness. Graceless husbands or wives can distress and ensnare those partners in life in whose souls God by His Spirit dwells.

In the night I was greatly affected by the words: "...for there the Lord commanded the blessing, even life for evermore". (*Ps.* 133: 3) Many wish me 'a happy New Year'; but this word from the lips of the Lord, at the dawn of the year, has made me happy beyond what I can tell.

January 4, 1955

Reading again Thomas Goodwin on the work of the Holy Spirit. None of the Puritans has the tremendous sweep of Goodwin. His magnificent trail casts more light on the theological truths which he handled than any other. Owen is massive; Manton is rich in ideas; Howe is deep and clear; but Goodwin's mind is expansive, spontaneous and heavenly.[26]

This morning I awoke with the words, "...forget not all His benefits". (*Ps.* 103: 2) By this word the Lord would have me be thankful for an unceasing flow of mercies, instead of my becoming fretful and complaining over His wise withholdings and just denials. It takes grace to be content with such things as we have: with the Cross, as with the cup of kindness and comfort.

Our dear daughter, Anne, has returned to Glasgow. In asking the Lord to give her good success in her work as a nurse I was curiously arrested by these words, "Thou preparedst room before [her]". (*Ps.* 80: 9) Time may tell what the words mean.

26 Murdo Campbell showed a particular affinity with the English Puritans.

January 18, 1955

Our Church Officer is dying: a physically strong man struck down. I visited him, and prayed; the Lord, I think, was there.

Awoke the next morning with the words, "Then they are glad because they be quiet; so he bringeth them unto their desired haven". (*Ps.* 107: 30) I felt that certain of His people were now at rest. Later, I attended the funerals of two men, one of whom was the Church Officer. They both lived, I believe, in the fear of the Lord. Afterwards I was refreshed by the words, "For a great door and effectual is opened unto me, and there are many adversaries". (1 *Cor.* 16: 9)

March 8, 1955

Had been at two Communions in the island of Lewis. The strain of preaching to such crowds for twelve consecutive days is great. At one, as I was addressing the Lord's Table from the words "Whom having not seen ye love" (1 *Peter* 1: 8), a wave of this love swept for a moment or two over my heart. I was embarrassed in having to pause until I could regain my composure and my speech. At the other, there was an unusual solemnity about the services. God 'opened my mouth' on Sabbath evening when I preached from *John* 3: 16. The "pillar of cloud" (*Ex.* 13: 21) is still over our congregations in Lewis. 'The Lord is there." (*Ezek.* 48: 35)[27]

March 25, 1955

Another bright light is extinguished in this once-favoured parish. Mr John MacFarquhar, my senior Elder in Resolis, is gone. He was the last of a band of elders in the Black Isle who had been in touch with spiritually better days. Our talks together led me to appreciate this good man's uncommon nearness to the Lord and his secret life of prayer. He longed for the day when the Lord shall again "rend the heavens and... come down". (*Is.* 64: 1)

27 'The wave of spiritual power which swept over Lewis in the great revival of 1818-1829 has, in fact, not yet spent itself.' (M 9) This revival was a late flowering of the wider Evangelical Revival.

April 2, 1955

The glorious prospect of the Millennium Age, and of the coming of the Lord, give me much comfort. The last three verses of Psalm 96 seldom fail to touch my heart. "Let the heavens rejoice, and let the earth be glad; let the sea roar, and the fullness thereof. Let the field be joyful, and all that is therein: then shall all the trees of the wood rejoice before the Lord: for he cometh to judge the earth: he shall judge the world with righteousness, and the people with his truth."

A few years ago, in the island of Skye, I heard these words sung with great power and solemnity. I had entered the Church at dusk, as the minister was finishing the sermon. In the gathering darkness one of the finest voices one could hear began precenting these words in Gaelic. The Lord gave me a glimpse, through the bright vistas of prophetic time, of that day when His rest in the Church shall be glorious, and when His coming "with clouds" shall be hailed by His redeemed. (*Rev.* 1: 7)

April 4, 1955

Last night, surveying my past labours in God's vineyard, I fell into great distress. Tried to comfort myself by enumerating the known conversions which took place under my ministry, but this failed to bring any comfort since my sheaves were so few, and my nets so empty. Afterwards I felt I had been guilty of presumption as 'the Day' alone will declare every man's work. (*Joel* 3: 14) In prayer I pleaded the promise of "the great door and effectual" which the Lord has set before me. (1 *Cor.* 16: 9) He came very near to me in the words, "The steps of a good man are ordered by the Lord". (*Ps.* 37: 23) But alas, I now feel so far from God both in my thoughts and affections.

May 14, 1955

Called on Rev Mr MacLachlan, the Free Church minister at Maryburgh, Ross-shire, who let me see a Fragment of a Diary written by a cultured young lady, Miss Jessie Thain, one of Robert Murray M'Cheyne's converts. These recollections of a young but fragrant life carry with them a 'M'Cheyne' atmosphere. This ailing young lady was so knit to M'Cheyne in the love of Christ that after he passed away her heart was broken. Yet her remarks on this subject are dignified and most spiritual. The intensity of the affection which her remarks disclose is a true, if often a painful, characteristic of the gracious soul. This precious Diary should really be in print.[28]

Had sweet moments of late in private prayer in the Church vestry. The doors were shut to other people, but He was there.

Was told of the conversion of a student I met when lecturing at Alloa, Clackmannanshire, and that her presence at the Church services has encouraged the Lord's people. My soul rejoices. To lead one precious soul to Christ is worth a thousand worlds.

May 26, 1955

Reading this morning Isaiah 51. Memory brought back seasons when portions of this chapter came with light and refreshment to my spirit. One of these was in Rogart, Sutherland, when Rev Prof John MacLeod, D.D., the Free Church College Principal, preached from the words, "Awake, awake... O arm of the Lord; awake, as in the ancient days..." (*Is.* 51: 9) Our Highlands once enjoyed days of God's right hand. We are now in the midst of much spiritual desolation; but if the feet of the Blessed One were to pass again through our land the desert would soon blossom as the rose. But few mourn His absence or cry with His Church, "Saw ye him whom my soul loveth?" (*Songs* 3: 3)[29]

28 *The Diary of Jessie Thain*, edited by the Revd Murdoch Campbell, 1955
29 'I was asked to conduct services in one of the nearer South-Western Isles where we had a few small congregations. This once-favoured isle was, over a century ago, the scene of a fruitful evangelical revival. Now it had almost become a mere holiday resort.' (M 96)

June 1, 1955

Sleep fled from my eyes last night. I had a disturbing sense of having neglected my private devotions through absence from home. But the Lord was gracious in giving me a blessing, and a refreshing sleep in the morning. On awakening, the precious words, "His name shall endure for ever ... and men shall be blessed in him, and all nations shall call him blessed", were in my mouth. (*Ps.* 72: 17)

For some days now I had access to the Lord in prayer for the day when His glory shall cover the earth. I may not see that blessed time except by faith and afar off. But the comfort of the promise is sweet.

June 9, 1955

This morning in reading the 31st Chapter in *Jeremiah* I saw anew the marvel of God's everlasting love for His people. Words of rebuke and threatenings follow each other like rolling thunders through the whole of this prophecy. But through all one may hear the "still small voice" of God's covenant love. (1 *Kings* 19: 12) O! the infinite kindness of God in identifying Himself in mercy with poor sinful men. This is an unceasing wonder. He never wearies of the countless number who, in every generation, seek to touch the hem of His garment, and who wait at His door begging for bread. And at His door none ever perished.

June 16, 1955

"To the hungry soul every bitter thing is sweet." (*Pr.* 27: 7) It is thus with me today.

On Thursday morning I awoke with the words, "Simon, Simon, Satan desired to have you, that he may sift you as wheat; but I have prayed for thee..." (*Luke* 22: 31) I had been praying in my sleep, and these were the words with which I ended. To be forewarned is to be forearmed. Whatever the words may imply, I put myself under the protecting care of the Most High.

July 6, 1955

Assisted at Communions. Had the painful experience of enjoying mental freedom while my heart was unmoved, and while those who listened were apparently also untouched by the holy fire of Christ's love. One does not wish for mere emotion; but a house without a fire is comfortless. If the heart fails to kindle into flame we remain cold and unresponsive. Yet I met some tender souls in each place who did seem affected by the Word.

Had been praying much in my sleep of late. Though I often awake with the words of God on my lips, this is a new experience. On each occasion I awoke as soon as my prayer ended. Last night I ended my praying with the words, "He which hath begun a good work in you will perform it until the day of Jesus Christ". (*Phil.* 1: 6) Can it be that this is from the Spirit of grace and supplications; and that God both gives and hears these prayers? "I sleep but my heart waketh." (*Songs* 5: 2) I awake out of these sweet frames refreshed by the love of Jesus.

Yesterday the Lord again refreshed my spirit in this way by waking me with the words, "And they that be wise shall shine as the brightness of the firmament; and they that turn many to righteousness as the stars for ever and ever". (*Dan.* 12: 3) Though I could not make a personal application of this great promise I was comforted by the thought that in the world to come I may, by His forgiveness and peace, share in the glory which shall be revealed in all His people.

Our good and sweet daughter, Mary, has passed in all her school examinations, and like an uncaged nightingale she fills the home with songs!

July 12, 1955

Home after a visit to Glenmoriston. The natural aspect of this lovely glen is unchanged; but many of my dear friends in the Lord are gone. The Communion season was a refreshing occasion. Had a glimpse of one of my 'Bethels', where I once spent many hours wrestling with the Angel. At Fort Augustus I visited our first child's grave. I was supported by the assurance that his soul is with Christ in glory. The Lord revealed this to me, as I wept for him on the crest of a hill several years after his death, through the words, "In my Father's house are many mansions; if it were not so I would have told you". (*John* 14: 2)

July 25, 1955

Awoke this morning on the lap of a great comfort. Gradually I realised that something inconceivably sweet had, as it were, flooded my spirit. I found myself quoting the last three verses of Psalm 96, words which I particularly love.[30] The very afterglow of this kindly beam of heavenly comfort left me happy all day.

August 2, 1955

On a short holiday at Gairloch, Wester Ross, in ideal weather. Yesterday evening I stood for an hour at nearby Opinan admiring the play of light and shade on the rising moorland, and on the distant hills. Could not help associating the scene with Him Whose feet were "beautiful". (*Songs* 7: 1) Tried to envisage the hour when He shall come again over "the mountains of Bether". (*Songs* 2: 17) Much affected by this blessed hope. My love, I felt, transcended the barriers of time and space to embrace anew the adorable Redeemer in Heaven.

August 6, 1955

Today the words, "...except the Lord keep the city, the watchman waketh but in vain" (*Ps.* 127: 1) came as a seasonable reminder that the battle is lost if the Mighty One is not my Help. Be Thou my Shield.

Back in Resolis. Felt that if our house could speak it would say, 'Welcome home!'

30 "Let the heavens rejoice, and let the earth be glad; let the sea roar, and the fullness thereof. Let the field be joyful, and all that is therein: then shall all the trees of the wood rejoice before the Lord: for he cometh to judge the earth: he shall judge the world with righteousness, and the people with his truth."

August 9, 1955

Today I received intimation from Edinburgh that I had been elected Moderator of the next General Assembly. Was quite alarmed by the information. Went to the Lord in prayer, and was reminded of a Scripture which was present with me the previous night. It took me some time before I could see its relevance to my own case. But I shall further wait on the Lord before committing myself on such a responsible and solemn issue. The immediate effect of this news was to fill me with disquiet and anxiety.

August 23, 1955

Had a melting view, in secret, of the goodness of God. Could not but praise Him that He is the God that He is. Found it pleasant to think that over the vast dominions of the universe God reigns. And His eyes are ever upon His own. Therefore all is well with those who love Him.

September 13, 1955

Had been reading 'Rabbi' Duncan and Dr M'Crie on the grace of assurance. The former makes the highest pinnacle of this grace to consist in the communication of the Divine mind to the soul by means of the written Word; but, wisely, the good man says nothing about the variety of ways in which God does this. Dr M'Crie moves severely on one line, deprecating God's more intimate dealings with His people. But God's wisdom is manifold. Although the Lord's people meet at so many points His dealings with them are varied and sometimes mysterious. But I was quite upset lest my own assurance may not be faith's true offspring. I went to pray with the heart-rending question on my lips, "Art thou he that should come, or look we for another?" (*Mat.* 11: 3) But the Lord rebuked me for casting any reflection on His former kindness, and for giving way to the vile sin of unbelief. Prayed afterwards to be restored and forgiven. Let me draw all my light and comfort from the Bible, and not from the comments of men, however correct and valuable in themselves.

September 30, 1955

Gave assistance at Communions. Though I found it a pleasant task to preach to the people many seemed to be 'Gospel hardened'. In secret, afterwards, I had a sore heart thinking how often Christ had to leave His dwelling-place on earth because of the sins of those who profess to love Him. No greater calamity could overtake us than that the Beloved should withdraw Himself. Alas for the Church: its chambers are dark and cold; and for the world: its judgment is at the door.

October 3, 1955

Our daughter, Mary, is leaving for Aberdeen University. Grace has heightened and refined her natural gentleness. Now as she leaves the shelter and safety of her home my prayers shall follow her. May the Lord fashion her into one of His jewels, that in her generation she may reflect His beauty and adorn His doctrine.

Came in from the services this evening sad at heart and weary in body. Instead of the Lord's smile on my public work He is like One who hears not my prayers. This is one of the "hard things" in my lot, and in that of others. (*Ps.* 60: 3) "We see not our signs." (*Ps.* 74: 9)

October 4, 1955

A fit of unbelief made me tremble lest the Lord should desert me in the comfort and enlightenment of His precious word. Blessed be His Name that He did not mark iniquity; for early this morning He spoke to my soul in the words of Psalm 103 v. 14, "For he knoweth our frame; he remembereth that we are dust". The compassion and love of the Lord for His frail, erring people are what I particularly saw in these words. Do they also announce the death of an acquaintance?

October 18, 1955

The words, "Let integrity and uprightness preserve me", refreshed my soul this day. (*Ps.* 25: 21) Six years ago the Lord met me in these words; and His reminding me of them seems to contain a clear light as to how I should keep His way. May it please Him so to carry me safely through every danger.

October 29, 1955

For several days now I have been very conscious of God's sweet peace dwelling in my heart. Provocations were placed in my path, but my spirit remained calm, for the Day Star was in view. When He gives quietness who can make trouble? Let me, however, watch and pray, "for this is not [my] rest". (*Micah* 2: 10)

Home from Communion services. Felt that as usual, it was light and shade; but the Lord may bless His word unknown to us.

November 2, 1955

Found myself unnecessarily anxious over my temporal circumstances. And yet all my needs are supplied day by day. Instead of leaving the vague day that we call tomorrow in God's hand we begin to live it before it arrives, and to envisage troubles which shall never likely arise. This is a great evil. The Lord very sweetly corrected me in the word: "Trust ye in the Lord for ever". (*Is.* 26:4) Let me therefore repose in His faithfulness and goodness.

November 15, 1955

Reading the life of Halyburton. The account he gives of his conversion, as if a golden light from Heaven had streamed into his mind and heart, is in keeping with the experience of Paul, as well as of men such as Jonathan Edwards, Dr. Love and David Brainerd. This wonderful apprehension of spiritual realities, and of the glorious Persons who inhabit eternity, was a passing out of darkness into light. How few there are, myself included, on whose souls the Sun of Righteousness arises with such brightness and consolation. It is hard to live in a perpetual spiritual twilight with only fleeting glimpses of the glory of Christ.

December 10, 1955

In seeking to make my requests known to God in secret prayer, my mind is apt to dwell on certain issues pertaining to personal needs and the needs of God's Cause. Is it necessary to continue day after day asking the Lord the same things; or is it better to present our plea and retire, leaving Him to answer in His own time and way? Apart from the unutterable sweetness of communion with the Lord in prayer, I think "continuing instant in prayer" is more Scriptural. (*Rom.* 12: 12) Our needs are continuous, and our enemies never retire to winter quarters. Therefore "men ought *always* to pray". (*Luke* 18:1) When I was tempted to sit still and wait for the Lord to answer the prayers of the past months He met me in the words, "Ask, and it shall be given you; seek, and ye shall find; knock, and it shall be opened unto you". (*Mat.* 7: 7) In this way I was both encouraged and corrected.

December 21, 1955

A letter from one of my Elders in Glasgow. My love for my old congregations of Fort Augustus and Partick Highland increases with the years. It is strange that I should have awakened this morning before the letter came, singing the words:
"How lovely is thy dwelling place,
O Lord of hosts to me:
The tabernacles of thy grace,
How pleasant Lord they be." (*Ps.* 84: 1)

A wave of nostalgia passed over my spirit as the significance of these words came before my mind. They also brought with them sad and sweet recollections of other days.

December 23, 1955

A sweet drop of the love of Jesus was let fall into my poor soul this afternoon. Through the day I felt unnecessarily agitated; and when in prayer I lifted up my heart to God He met me in the words: "O thou afflicted, tossed with tempest, and not comforted, behold, I will lay thy stones with fair colours, and lay thy foundations with sapphires". (*Is.* 54: 11) This composing word was followed by another which greatly calmed my spirit: "Thou in thy mercy hast led forth the people which thou has redeemed". (*Ex.* 15: 13)

The Revd and Mrs Campbell, Tarbert, Harris, circa 1956

1956

February 8, 1956

Much exhausted and weary after the Communion in Inverness; but the Lord be praised for the news that my words there were blessed to some. Today I was refreshed by the words, "But God is the strength of my heart". (*Ps.* 73: 26) And I am also literally stronger since then.

February 15, 1956

Today, a lovely word reached me from Mrs Watson, Springfield, Resolis who had "found honey" in the service on Sabbath evening. (1 *Sam.* 14: 29) And how pleasant can a Sabbath day be, especially in the home: God seems to come in with us, as if a golden ray from the Sun of Righteousness rested on our hearts.

February 24, 1956

For the last several days I was laid aside with fever and chest pains. The evening before I took ill, the Messianic words of David awoke me out of sleep: "I looked for some to take pity, but there was none; and for comforters, but I found none". (*Ps.* 69: 20) In my illness, surrounded by the affection and ministry of my wife and friends, my thoughts went out to Him Who had nowhere to lay His head, and Who in the awful agonies of death was forsaken of all. No man or angel ministered to Him then. The Father in Heaven forsook Him also in that hour. I could not but wonder at the infinite love of Christ Who was so forsaken that we might be for ever cherished and embraced of God.

March 24, 1956

Enjoyed an unusual degree of mental freedom on Sabbath. I spoke of Christ's love, but felt little enough of it in my soul. In the early morning I felt distressed through the words, "My flesh longs in a dry and thirsty land, wherein no waters be". (*Ps.* 63: 1) Poor Resolis, will ever "showers of blessing" gladden thy borders again? (*Ezek.* 34: 26)

On Thursday I attended the funeral here of a very worldly man. A fleet of cars extended for half a mile behind his remains, honouring the dead. If only he, and so many who stood by his cold grave, honoured God by attending His house. There are many whose minds and affections are buried in the earth and its cares long before their bodies are laid in the dust. What an unspeakably sad end this is for an *immortal* soul!

April 14, 1956

My old friend Rev A. A. MacDonald, formerly Free Church minister of Bracadale, in Skye, has gone to his eternal rest. He was a simple, childlike man who knew the Lord since boyhood. Love and holiness clothed him as a garment.

Today I enjoyed a lovely walk on the upper Springfield road in Resolis. The warm sun was shining out of the sky and my soul was gladdened by rays from the Sun of Righteousness. Felt it good to meditate on the perfect balance between God's sovereignty in the salvation of His people, and their own felt responsibility and sense of urgency in making their calling and election sure. Only they reach the distant desired haven, who row evenly with these two oars!

April 27, 1956

I am now over twenty-five years in the ministry; and to mark the occasion, as well as my appointment as Moderator of the General Assembly, the people here have given my wife and myself very generous gifts.

Retired to rest with memories which brought much sadness. In the early morning, however, the Lord consoled my mind through the first verse of Psalm 27: "The Lord is my light and my salvation: whom shall I fear? the Lord is the strength of my life; of whom shall I be afraid?" The weeping of the night He changed into a morning of joy.

Praying more deliberately for God's help in *little* things, and unless I am deceived, the results are wonderful. Oh, that I had the wisdom to put the Lord before me in *all* things!

May 1, 1956

A little girl of seven years asked me why we do not see Jesus with our bodily eyes. I explained that Jesus lives in our heart, and although we do not see Him, we feel His presence with us, and hear Him speak to us in His Word. 'But how could Jesus be in our heart and also in Heaven?' I tried to illustrate this by pointing to the sun in the sky and saying that if we turn our eyes to it, a little sun may be seen in our eyes too. In the same way when we look by faith to Jesus, the Sun of Righteousness, a perfect image of Him is formed in our hearts; and His love, light and life come into our hearts also. There is only one sun in the sky; but a million reflections of it may be seen in as many eyes. There is only one spiritual Sun, but all the Lord's people in Heaven, and on earth, reflect His glory. With this simple thought the child was very pleased and satisfied. May the Lord truly be her light and salvation.

May 7, 1956

Called on a parishioner who is dying. Before entering his home I sent up an 'arrow' prayer to the Lord to show me, if He so willed, how it fared with his soul. Before I left the house the words, "Thou art not far from the Kingdom of God", came with a softening power to my mind. (*Mark* 12: 34)

Our friend's daily walk down to the bridge beside the manse to collect his milk was an attractive part of our landscape.

May 31, 1956

Arrived home last night after the meetings of our General Assembly. The Lord graciously sustained me throughout all the tasks which devolved upon me as this year's Moderator. One member spoke of the 'uncanny calm' which brooded over us;

but to me it was the peace of God, and the manifestation of His restraining power in answer to many prayers. Our several visits to Holyrood House were pleasant, and I found the Lord High Commissioner and his Lady most kind and friendly. On arriving home my wife gave me a sprig of lily of the valley from our garden. Its beauty and sweet fragrance made me think of Him whose fragrance and loveliness make Heaven a place of everlasting delight. I am glad to say that when I awoke the following morning the Lord was very near me in His Word.

June 23, 1956

Death, which is so busy among us, dissolves all mere earthly relationships. But grace establishes new and sweeter ones, which last through eternal ages. Christ on the Cross dissolved the natural relationship between Himself and His mother according to the flesh, but as her Lord and Redeemer, He sealed the eternal union between them in the bonds of grace and covenant love. His command to John concerning her shows that the tie between those who do God's will is tender and loving, and also impressed with the changeless seal of eternity. It is a source of infinite consolation to all His loved ones.

July 9, 1956

Returned from Edinburgh where I attended the Queen's Garden Party at Holyrood House. The Queen is a humble and very kind lady; but I felt that too heavy a burden is laid on her.

Came home feeling extremely fatigued, as I so often do. The Lord wrapped me however in the glorious promise of Psalm 91, v. 4, and my sleep was very restful and refreshing: "He shall cover thee with his feathers, and under his wings shalt thou trust: his truth shall be thy shield and buckler". Perhaps I should also appreciate more the fact that my sojourn, for the time being, is in the quiet and lovely hollow of Resolis.

July 14, 1956

Today in Resolis I stood looking at a large and flourishing field of corn waving in a warm summer breeze. Round its borders one could see the numberless smaller stalks which could not compare in strength or height with the rest. And yet they belonged to the field. Felt that I had utterly no desire to be anything, if I could only be the least and the lowliest in "the great congregation" which shall stand at last before God. (*Ps.* 22: 25) To be of the number in the Covenant of grace though for ever the least and the last among them. Lord, deepen my humility, and let me sit lowly at Thy feet.

August 7, 1956

Arrived home from a Communion in the isle of Harris refreshed in body and soul. The 'goings' of the Holy One were among us. It was a joy to speak to the people. In Scalpay isle He lifted up His hands above us and blessed us. Perhaps even more precious than our public services was the spiritual communion in the Manse.

August 26, 1956

Reading a little book by a converted Jewish lady of great intelligence. Her greatest discovery was that the world of Christian experience is a real world, perhaps the only real world. Those who enter it live in a new spiritual dimension, and make contact with God, who is the only and ultimate Reality. This is not a realm of cold abstraction or cloudy idealism but a warm realm whose light, love and glory enter our heart and consciousness. By the converting grace of God, our own souls become a new world within. In Christ we are new creations. As such we enter by faith and by communion with God into what the Bible calls "the heavenlies". When this happens the lower world around us takes on a new colour and we see it with new eyes. The curse seems to lift off the earth when we gaze upon it with the love of Christ in our hearts.

September 30, 1956

Returned from Glasgow where I gave the Address of Welcome to our School of Theology. My visit was rendered very pleasant through a closer acquaintance with Professor A. M. Renwick, of the Free Church College, who is truly a man of God. His child-like bearing, simple faith and warm responsive heart are unaffected by his powers and learning. His love to His Lord and His people is deep and constant.

October 10, 1956

Last night I returned from a Communion in Glasgow. On the Monday morning the words, "Be content with such things as ye have, for he hath said, I will never leave you nor forsake you", impressed themselves upon my mind. (*Heb.* 13: 5) Accordingly, I concluded my sermon on Monday by exhorting the Lord's people to study contentment in all trials and circumstances, since He will never, never forsake them.

October 20, 1956

Reading the private Diary of Cathie MacRae, a refined and godly girl from Lochalsh in Wester Ross, who died many years ago in the Maryburgh Sanatorium, in Ross-shire [31]. She died rejoicing in the Lord. The deep solace which those young women found in their religion makes impressive reading. One by one they were gently picked by the Lord's hand, as the gardener gathers his flowers, and transferred to the Garden above, where the inhabitant shall never say 'I am sick'. The love of those young women to the Redeemer was as tender as their sympathy and affection for one another. In her spiritual growth Cathie was greatly helped by Nurse Chrissie MacKenzie from Borve, Lewis, whom I knew well in my student days.

31 Before a vaccine for tuberculosis became available, the disease killed many previously healthy young women from the Highlands and Islands who left home for work, particularly in nursing.

November 11, 1956

During the last several days my sins have descended on me like swarms of unclean birds. Sinful thoughts have darkened my spirit. And where is my grief over my sin? No wonder, therefore, that He should confront me in the terrible words of Psalm 6, v. 1: "O Lord, rebuke me not in thine anger, neither chasten me in thy hot displeasure". Prayed earnestly that He might show mercy. This morning as I left my bedroom I was arrested by the words, "For the law of the Spirit of life in Christ Jesus has made me free from the law of sin and death". (*Rom.* 8: 2) I could then breathe in hope. But how can I arise with a "body of death" pressing me down to the dust? (*Rom.* 7: 24) May His grace be "sufficient" for me. (2 *Cor.* 12: 9)

November 23, 1956

Preached at Perth last Sabbath. At Braco, in Perthshire, I enjoyed an hour of Christian fellowship. Presided at a meeting of the Assembly's Commission. Now that I am home again I am so happy to find a rich blessing in Psalm 89, v. 15: "Blessed is the people that know the joyful sound: they shall walk, O Lord, in the light of thy countenance".

November 28, 1956

This afternoon I was arrested by the words of Psalm 90, v. 1: "Lord, though hast been our dwelling place in all generations". Afterwards as I walked toward Newmills, Resolis they powerfully affected my mind. They declare that we had a Home in God's love from all eternity: "before the mountains were brought forth". (*Ps.* 90: 2) We were chosen in Christ before the foundation of the world. This blessed conception of God as the Home of His people is woven into the experience of the Church "in all generations".

He was a Bethel to Jacob; a protecting Pillar to the Tribes; a secret Place to His holy dove. "O my dove, that art...in the secret places of the stairs." (*Songs* 2: 14) He is in every age and in every place "as a little sanctuary" to His people. (*Ezek.* 11: 16) And what a Home this is! Here are rest and peace. Here are joy and communion. Here we meet the whole family in Heaven and on earth. Here are the provisions of the Covenant of grace sealed and enjoyed. The best of all is that access into this happy Abode is through Christ and the blood of sprinkling. If we come this way we may read the word *WELCOME* on the Door.

December 24, 1956

Reading in the Book of *Deuteronomy*. Here one finds an awe-inspiring prediction of those calamities which throughout history have overtaken Israel. And how wonderfully does the prophecy dovetail into its fulfilment. The day will come, however, when Israel shall look upon Him Whom they have pierced. Lord, hasten the time.

1957

January 4, 1957

Enjoyed a blessing this morning in the words: "Thou shalt be in league with the stones of the field". (*Job* 5: 23)

The thought that the forces of the universe are 'reconciled' to those who are reconciled to God in Christ I found very pleasant and reassuring. All things are under the immediate control of Christ who has given commandment to save us. (*Ps.* 71: 3) Most of the fears which beset God's people have therefore their source in unbelief or ignorance. Well might we ask with David, "Why art thou cast down, O my soul? And why art thou disquieted within me? Hope thou in God". (*Ps.* 42: 15) However adverse God's providence may appear in relation to the Church, or the believer personally, its final end is their preservation. How wonderfully is this brought out, for example, in the Book of *Esther*. There we see the irony of Providence in a way before which the powers of this world should tremble.

February 28, 1957

Last Sabbath I broadcast a sermon in Gaelic from Glasgow on the words, "I know that my redeemer liveth". (*Job* 19: 25) I began in much anxiety, but almost at once felt the Lord was beside me, so that all my fears vanished. May the Lord bless the Word to some of the invisible multitude whom I addressed.

March 8, 1957

A lovely soul-satisfying word has brought cheer and life to my discouraged soul. "I the Lord will keep it; I will water it every moment: lest any hurt it, I will keep it night and day." (*Is.* 27: 3) Since my fears and needs are so great I made a personal application of this passage. Perhaps also the Lord is watching over my congregation, and is silently blessing some.

March 9, 1957

Visited our devoted and gracious Resolis Elder, Mr Robert Grigor, who is very unwell. His face shone as he told us of his trust in Christ. Prayed afterwards that this good man, if the Lord so wills, might be spared to us. He is a man of great good sense and charity, two qualities perhaps rarely found in the one person.

March 15, 1957

Early this morning I dreamt that I was in the company of my late father and mother. The room we sat in was flooded with a warm light. In my dream I sang the first verse of Psalm 40: "I waited for the Lord; and he inclined unto me, and heard my cry". I felt myself passing through a barrier of sin and sorrow into a state of great peace. It was only a dream, but one not without meaning; perhaps it was a foretaste of freedom from sin and pain, in Heaven, where they see Christ's face with joy.

March 18, 1957

Our Elder, Mr Robert Grigor, passed on yesterday to, as I sincerely believe, his everlasting rest. He was mine own son in the faith. It is only about five years since he came to know the Lord. Since then the Cause of Christ was the subject of his interest and prayers. He was one of the most useful, the most peaceable, and the most affectionate office-bearers I have worked with. All my memories of him are tender and endearing. On his death-bed he was happy. The enemy pursued his soul to the end but, in his words, "I had a hold of Christ, and he fled". Three hours before he died, as I was looking toward his home in Springfield, Resolis the heart-rending words came before my mind: "And the place thereof shall know it no more". (*Ps.* 103: 16) But we believe that, though absent here, he is now "with Christ; which is far better". (*Philippians* 1: 23)

April 8, 1957

At 1.00 a.m. on a recent morning I awoke in a sweet frame with the words, "The daughter of Tyre shall be there with a gift". (*Ps.* 45: 12) I wondered what this word could mean, until the post arrived with news of a legacy to forward the work of the Lord in the congregation. The lady who left this money once resided in this district, but I never met her. Another lady met me on the road and told me that her late sister had left us money for the same purpose.

April 20, 1957

Was much refreshed in reading again the wonderful story, which is also a perfect literary gem, of Abraham's servant and his prayerful dependence on God for constant guidance. (*Gen.* 24) This unnamed man had a degree of spirituality and nearness to God seldom found in this world.

May 8, 1957

Home after a round of engagements in London, Cardiff and Perth. In Cardiff I met Rev E. J. Poole-Connor, founder in 1922 of the Fellowship of Independent Evangelical Churches, who remembered Charles Spurgeon.

May 14, 1957

Out walking, I could hear the wood pigeon in the distance, "the voice of the turtle" reminding us that summer is come. (*Songs* 2: 12) But in these parts the signs of a spiritual "dayspring from on high" are absent. (*Luke* 1: 78) This affected me much, and I could only retire to pray that God might visit us again in mercy. Overcome with sorrow knowing that I shall not live to see the coming days of blessedness, except as Moses saw the good land afar off. I can only pray with the Bride, "... turn, my Beloved, and be thou like a roe or a young hart upon the mountains of Bether". (*Songs* 2: 17)[32]

32 The Church past and future is often called 'the Bride of Christ'. A bride and groom however both expect to benefit from their relationship. In

Our Assembly meetings begin on Tuesday. Prepared a sermon for the opening day on 2 Corinthians 10, v. 4: "For the weapons of our warfare are not carnal, but mighty through God to the pulling down of strong holds". The Lord, I hope, has graciously encouraged me by applying to my mind the words of Psalm 66, v. 13: "I will go into thy house with burnt offerings: I will pay thee my vows". Lord, assist me in the solemn duties of Thy house.

June 2, 1957

A happy day. It is now over twenty-three years since the Lord gave me the promise that I would live to see my "children's children". (*Ps.* 128: 6) I had been several times since then brought almost to death's door. Lord, bless this little girl, and may she be a jewel in Thy Crown.

June 22, 1957

Felt revived through the words of Moses, "Make us glad according to the days wherein thou hast afflicted us, and the years wherein we have seen evil". (*Ps.* 90: 15) Do these words, although in themselves a prayer, imply a doctrine of compensation? Are the Lord's people compensated in this world for afflictions endured? Although the recompense is really enjoyed in eternity, many of the saints were given bright days after prolonged seasons of darkness and afflictions, and a calm sunset before the end. But there is no invariable rule, since God's dealings with His people, within the circle of Time, vary as His sovereign will sees fit.

---

contrast the command to 'love God and your neighbour as yourself' is altruistic or self-forgetting, connecting love to God and to your neighbour. "Inasmuch as ye have done it unto the least of these my brethren, ye have done it unto me." (*Mat.* 25:40)

July 22, 1957

Our summer Communion came to an end this day. Several precious sermons were preached, but the heavens remained as brass. After the last service I went into the Church and there, alone, I found Him Whom my soul loves. Lord, how is it that I do not get among men what I find when alone with Thee?

August 14, 1957

In Skye, was grieved at the apparent hardness of many; but some seemed to be under the dew of heaven, like Gideon's fleece. The Lord visited my soul there in the far-reaching promise of Psalm 113 v. 7: "He raiseth up the poor out of the dust".

In Lewis, as I visited my parents' and grandmother's graves, these words powerfully arrested my mind: "If ye then be risen with Christ, seek those things which are above, where Christ sitteth on the right hand of God". (*Col.* 2: 12) I had faith's view of them among the great multitude who stand before the Throne.

August 30, 1957

Home from Stornoway, isle of Lewis, where I assisted at the Communion. The crowds were overwhelming; but the Lord upheld me. On the Saturday night I had a curious sense of being sustained and surrounded by the prayers of many of God's people.

September 9, 1957

On a recent morning the words of Psalm 37, v. 37 impressed themselves very powerfully on my mind: "Mark the perfect man, and behold the upright: for the end of that man is peace". The same evening I heard of the death of a good man, with whom I once travelled in a train. I still recall the depth of affection with which he bade me farewell at the station in Glasgow, and the lovely words he quoted as we parted.

September 18, 1957

I have been greatly saddened in remembering the days of old, and the years of His right hand. I remember the wonderful night when the Lord filled my soul with His love, and when I would have died if I could only have retained the unspeakably sweet enjoyment. But if I have tasted of the stream, I hope to reach the Sea at last. I thank God also that rays from the Sun of Righteousness sometimes break through the curtain of gloom which so often covers my spirit.

September 23, 1957

For several days I have been refreshed in thinking of the "treasure hid in a field", and the joy which its discovery gave to the finder. (*Mat.* 13, v. 44) This treasure is "the Kingdom of God" - an expression which embraces Christ, the Gospel, the promises, and the indwelling graces of the Spirit. It is hid in the field of Scripture, and when we find it we hide it in our hearts. "Blessed are the undefiled in the way, who walk in the law of the Lord." (*Ps.* 119: 1) Some have lighted on this heavenly Treasure as if by accident. The woman of Samaria found it unexpectedly at the Well of Sychar. Some who, in their unbelief and atheism, did not believe it was there to find, were led to it in a day of grace. Others found it after prolonged and despairing seeking. I recall the day when, sitting in a pew in Greenock, the eyes of my soul were opened to see it. That was an hour of joy, when God caused me to laugh, and the Almighty made my heart glad. (*Gen.* 21:6) I could then, like Moses and Paul, sell all that I might win Christ. Lord, may I, unworthy, be the means of leading others to see the infinite value of Christ, Who is the Treasure of all Thy people, and the Pearl of great price.

September 30, 1957

Discussing the hope of our Lord's second coming with a few of my fellow ministers. But on this subject we were a divided camp. I tried to plead for the post-millennial view which, I think, is both Scriptural and spiritual. It is also a view which offers no violence to the Christian consciousness. When the Lord's people pray with David for the day when, through the outpouring of the Spirit and the universal spread of the Gospel, His glory shall fill the whole earth, they find themselves on congenial ground. Besides, the great plea of the Lord's Prayer, "Thy Kingdom come. Thy will be done on earth, as it is in heaven", points in this direction. (*Mat.* 6: 10) The Lord clearly teaches that we should pray for the blessed age when this earth, on which Christ died, shall be a reflection of heaven, and when no opposition shall be offered to His holy will "in all places of his dominion". (*Ps.* 103: 22) But whatever view we hold on this subject we should love all who love His appearing.

October 10, 1957

Two booklets have come into my hand dealing with the philosophies behind Communism. I am convinced that Communism is Satan's imitation of the millennium, that is, of God's new age for a redeemed and purified world. The picture it gives us of a world of hideous uniformity, with human personality virtually destroyed, is most appalling. It envisages a world from which God is banished. But it is not to be: "The Lord *doth* reign". "He that sitteth in the heavens shall laugh: the Lord shall have them in derision." (Psalm 2)

Many are alarmed at the appearance of the Soviet space satellite over our planet. I cannot conceive of God's allowing man to defile, even with his physical presence, other worlds which may be untouched by evil.

November 23, 1957

Had occasion to write an ailing but Christless friend on the danger and folly of judging the quality and worth of the Gospel by its reflection in the lives of many who profess the Lord. No man, however holy, is consistent in every part of his conduct. Where one man is weak, another is strong. Yet we nurse deep resentments against many for their shortcomings as if we ourselves were perfect. This is how the evil one ensnares us. Reminded my friend that a settled evil resentment in the mind is a condition which Heaven cannot endure, and which hell cannot cure. Only the entrance of Christ's love can dissolve this evil of our heart and help us to live in the higher dimension of peace with God and good will toward all men.

November 28, 1957

I should more warmly thank God for His promises and more earnestly plead for their fulfilment. Some of His promises He honours immediately in our daily life, but most are related to the eternal future. Jacob's words, "and thou saidst", was faith keeping God to His Word. (*Gen.* 32: 12) In this exercise of faith there is deep assurance, reverence and joy, but no presumption.

December 23, 1957

The transition from the state of sin to grace can be swift and unbelievably sweet in its surprise. Does this not also suggest the soul's instant transition from grace to glory? For there is a greater spiritual distance between the state of sin and death and the state of life and reconciliation with God, than between grace here and glory in Heaven.

December 27, 1957

Several times of late I asked the Lord to "shew me a token for good". (*Ps.* 86: 17) My askings, I felt, were not very spiritual. God could have laid His sore rod on me for this. Instead I was corrected very tenderly in a dream in which a late beloved elder in Glasgow said that the greatest token for good that the Lord can show us is the Cross of Calvary, and the witness of His Spirit in our hearts that we are His. "My reins also instruct me in the night seasons." (*Ps.* 16: 7)

1958

January 1, 1958

Yesterday as I was again seeking to put myself and mine under the care of the ever-watchful Guardian of Israel the words, "And they shall be mine, saith the Lord of hosts, in that day when I make up my jewels", were applied to my mind in much assurance. (*Mal.* 3: 17) The previous evening one of my favourite promises touched my spirit in an unusual way: "This God is our God for ever: he will guide us even unto (or through) death". (*Ps.* 48: 14) Today, on the other hand, the Psalmist's prayer gave me much food for thought. "Create in me a clean heart, O God." (*Ps.* 51: 10) Vile sin "fills my loins with pain". (*Ps.* 38: 7) But I am thankful for the least desire after righteousness since this is, I hope, an earnest that "the Lord will perfect that which concerneth me". (*Ps.* 138: 8)

January 22, 1958

In reading the *Epistle to the Romans* I felt again quite astonished at its sheer spiritual sublimity. It is like a great mountain, the heights of which are wrapped in the mystery of God's predestinating will, and His sovereign love in Christ. The apostle begins at the base of the mountain, as it were, where all men are helplessly bogged in sin and guilt. But the ascent to the summit is glorious, for all God's redemptive acts are seen to revolve round the Person and Righteousness of the God-Man. Imputed righteousness, and justification by faith in Christ, are the two keys which provide us with an entrance into its secrets. From the pinnacle of God's love to the Church in Christ, the apostle enjoys a blessed view of the eternal safety of the elect. His descent by the other side of the mountain leads as it were into the valley of Christian duty and love, where, whatever trials await us, all is fair, pleasant and kind.

May 19, 1958

During a visit to Aberdeen I addressed a meeting of the University Evangelical Union. There was a good attendance of students from all the Faculties. The questions which emerged in the discussion afterwards would almost embarrass a Plato and Calvin rolled into one! My subject was 'Christ's obedience unto Death'.

In Glasgow, I had the rare experience of listening to a sweet melody which seemed to be within my own spirit.

June 16, 1958

Our short holiday in Skye was very enjoyable. The weather was kind, and the island looked lovely in its unique natural charms. My visit was made memorable through meeting two young friends who had been praying that the Lord might send someone into their company who would show them the way of Salvation. I could not describe the joy of speaking to them about the Good Part, and of leading them to the Well of Life. Eternity seemed to enter into our sweet fellowship. I left them in a state of quiet happiness with their hearts resting in the Lord. May the Holy Spirit reveal to them more of the loveliness of the Redeemer. Lord, watch over these Thy babes and lambs!

From Skye I travelled to assist at a friend's Communion. The Lord was kind to me in secret; for the words, "They looked unto him, and were lightened" greatly refreshed me. (*Ps.* 34: 5) Perhaps the measure of freedom which I enjoyed on Sabbath evening was a token that the Word found its way into some heart. The peace of God seemed to rest on the home of my friend.

June 22, 1958

This morning on my way to Inverness, I hope the Lord gave me a blessing. At least, I was conscious of much tenderness of heart as I mused on the words of Psalm 16 vs. 2-3: "...my goodness extendeth not to thee; But to the saints that are in the earth, and to the excellent, in whom is all my delight". Like Bunyan's 'Pilgrim' I was filled with a deep desire for more communion with the Lord and His people. We love His people because they are His. They are the subjects of His everlasting love, the purchase of His blood, and the people in whose hearts are His ways. His own image in them should endear them to our hearts. The felt spiritual kinship with them in their joys and sorrows is a lasting bond. My own life, necessarily isolated from many whom I dearly love in the Lord, is no doubt the poorer since I meet them so seldom. But an endless eternity together in the heavenly country shall make up for the brief denials of this life.

July 30, 1958

Attended our daughter Mary's graduation in Aberdeen. Listened to the long and dry speeches of the University orators; but on the whole it was an interesting occasion.

We had with us here at the Communion Rev Andrew Sutherland.[33] His holy and loving soul is ripening for the heavenly country. With us also at the Lord's Table was a dear English lad. How often do I thank God that within our many divisions His own dear people are to be found. Whatever their denominational badge they are united in love to Himself, to one another and in the inerrant truth of His holy Word.

August 15, 1958

Mr Spurgeon once said that he would rather go to Heaven by the grave, the way in which Christ and many of His people were brought, than after the manner of Elijah and Enoch. The grave is in itself a cold chamber, but when we enter it the Lord is there with us still. He redeemed our body also. Therefore when we lie down to sleep awhile in the grave our very flesh rests

33 The Revd Andrew Sutherland was minister of Duke Street (later known as Grant Street) Free Church, Glasgow from 1922 to 1941; Tobermory 1941 to 1945; and Glenshiel 1945 to 1951. He died in February, 1963.

in hope. He folds us in His love and promise. By lying there Himself He left it comfortable and fragrant for His people. Death cannot separate our bodies from the love of Christ. He will raise us up on the last day. So in death He bids us as it were 'Good night' until we meet Him again in the morning, when we shall be "satisfied with [his] likeness". (*Ps.* 17: 15)

This sweet truth should reconcile me to the temporary 'bed' where I shall one day lie down until the heavens (not 'Heaven') "be no more". (*Job* 14: 12)

August 29, 1958

Twice recently I awoke out of sleep with a delightful sense of Christ's love. I felt like a new man in a new world. Mental grief and heaviness were gone. But the blissful Presence soon left me, and to my very tears over His departure He was silent. The words, "Thou canst not see my face; for there shall no man see me, and live", came later with a solemn reminder that we cannot get in time what is reserved for us in the world to come. (*Ex.* 33: 20)

Pleaded afterwards with the Lord to help a young friend. These words were sealed on my spirit in much comfort: "But my faithfulness and my mercy shall be with him; and in my name shall his horn be exalted". (*Ps.* 89: 4) Lord, make him a candle within Thy Church on earth, and keep him faithful to Thy holy Word. His mind is keen and expansive; if the root of the matter is in him all is well.

October 9, 1958

Feeling happy, if somewhat exhausted, after a recent Communion in my native Isle. Whatever evils mar its reputation, Lewis has many people who exhibit true godliness, along with much spiritual and theological discernment. On Sabbath morning these words were present with me: "Verily, verily, I say unto you, the hour is coming, and now is, when the dead shall hear the voice of the Son of God: and they that hear shall live". (*John* 5: 25) The words came with such solemnity and power that I believe some did hear to their eternal advantage.

It was good to hear the voice of Donald MacLeod, one of my favourite precentors, in Scalpay isle.

Called today at Culbokie, in the Black Isle, to see an old man whose sweet remarks on the glory and the love of Christ filled me with wonder. He is 90 years old and ripe for glory, or so it seemed to me. How many of God's jewels lie hidden where they are known to few besides Himself?

November 12, 1958

A few days ago I was much impressed by the words, 'The heaven, even the heavens, are the Lord's: but the earth hath he given to the children of men". (*Ps.* 115: 16) The deep meaning and implication of these words seemed to flash on my mind. Man is now encroaching on part of the universe which properly and exclusively belongs to God. This is the spirit of Babel in another form. Not only will man be driven back to his earth, but the world itself which he has distressed and defiled by his sin shall be purged with fire. The proud and the wicked, to whom God and His Word are irrelevant, are reserved for that day. I am persuaded that the hour of His visitation is not far off.

December 10, 1958

On Friday afternoon, when I was in my room alone, the Lord broke through my darkness and deadness and gave me a brief Bethel season of His presence which, when accompanied by His love and Word, can transform the most distressing situation into a delightsome suburb of Heaven.

In Aberdeen I listened to a reproduction of my voice on a tape recorder, both in speech and song. I could hardly believe that the slow, deliberate Highland voice was really mine! Our real self eludes us.

December 15, 1958

In the duty of prayer I am always ready to halt; but the Lord Who is gracious and merciful is easily entreated. Several times of late He smiled on my prayer. I was very conscious of His aid in pleading for the revival of His Zion and the destruction of the Kingdom of darkness. Sometimes when I pray in this way I have an awareness that I am not alone, that many others in various parts of the earth are also pleading with God. This is the true communion of saints in this world. How inconceivably pleasant it is to share in the faith, joy and sufferings of the rest of God's family in this way. And woe to me if I do not pray at this time.

December 27, 1958

Recently the Lord in much kindness came to relieve and also, I hope, to reassure me. He applied His balm in these words, "The sacrifices of God are a broken spirit". (*Ps.* 51: 17) And, "Iniquities prevail against me: as for our transgressions, thou shalt purge them away". (*Ps.* 65: 3) Later the words, "Blessed is the people that know the joyful sound" also came with great comfort to my soul. (*Ps.* 89: 15) I was then able to see the connection between these passages. Who can speak like God?

1959

January 10, 1959

My mind was restless for a day or two, but this morning I was much affected by the words, "Thou wilt keep him in perfect peace, whose mind is stayed on Thee". (*Is.* 26: 3) But apart from the final rest in Heaven is there such a haven of peace for the soul? The words "perfect peace" might be translated, 'peace, peace'. There is the peace which we sometimes enjoy in communion with God, so beautifully expressed in Psalm 91 for example. A difficulty I find is to prevent sin and Satan from casting their malignant shadows over more serene moments, and from marring the enjoyment of God's peace within.

The other morning in prayer I began by quoting the Lord's Prayer. I was at once touched by its deep spirituality and marvellous comprehensiveness. Only God could compose such a prayer. Each phrase seemed to open a door into a new devotional world. All its pleas are abidingly relevant and appropriate. As the context shows it is meant to be a secret prayer, used only by God's people.

March 16, 1959

Drove to assist at the Communion in Kilmallie, Inverness-shire. This once-favoured part of Christ's vineyard has undergone a great change. The older witnesses are all away. On Sabbath morning I preached from a favourite theme, "Unto him that loved us..." (*Rev.* 1: 5)

On my way home I saw our child's grave at Fort Augustus. The flowers still grow over his little bed, where he sleeps "till the heavens be no more". (*Job* 14: 12) I hope to see him in that country where God shall wipe away my tears.

Afterwards I spent a few moments in the church where I began my ministry. An awe rested on my spirit as I stood in the pulpit, and as the solemn responsibilities of my office overwhelmed my mind. I can only hope that the perfect ministry and obedience of the Son of God cover the defects of mine.

March 30, 1959

Arrived home after spending ten days in hospital. God rendered my stay there memorable and pleasant through my conversations with a young person who was in depths of spiritual distress, but to whom the Lord gave a glorious and instant deliverance through the seasonable application of the words, "I, even I am he that blotteth out thy transgressions". (*Is.* 43: 25) Though weak in my body, as I wrestled for this precious soul God sealed this great promise of forgiveness in the words, "Set me as a seal upon thine heart, as a seal upon thine arm...". (*Song of Solomon* 8, v. 6) Her soul tasted of Christ's forgiveness as she pleaded with God in the prayer of David,

"My sins and faults of youth
Do thou O Lord forget;
After thy mercy think on me,
And for thy goodness great." (*Ps.* 25, v.7)

All other joys known to men are poor compared with that of leading a soul to Christ. It was one of the joys set before Himself, that of pardoning the poor sinner. Angels rejoice in this also. When a sinner weeps at the footstool of mercy, Heaven is full of smiles. Lord, I leave this little lamb in Thy care.

April 3, 1959

My article in the Free Church *Record* on the Christian's relation to nuclear warfare has aroused considerable comment in many quarters. I wrote it as a kind of corrective to the anti-war demonstrations now taking place all over the country.

My heart rejoiced when I was told of a young man from Skye who seems to have been converted through a talk I had with him on a journey. Lord, bless this lad, and make him one of Thy witnesses in his generation.

May 24, 1959

Met a friend on the way to Edinburgh. I find that my Christian love for my spiritual children is deep and tender and, I believe, exceeds the instinctive love of a mother for her child. Was led to pray for this soul that God may protect His child from the Adversary.

May 27, 1959

Preached a Gaelic service in the Aberdeen University Chapel. About seventy were present. Spoke extempore and with ease on the words, "Whereas I was blind, now I see". (*John* 9: 25) Professor Donald M. MacKinnon, of the Moral Philosophy Department, is very keen that David, our son, should take the Honours Course. I could offer no objection to this, especially since David appears to have a liking for philosophical subjects. The Professor looked quite an oddity. His mental intensity shows itself in a somewhat restless stare. But his conversation was easy and courteous.

This morning I awoke greatly refreshed by the words of Psalm 139 v. 8: "If I ascend up into heaven, thou art there; if I make my bed in hell, behold, thou art there." My soul seemed to entwine itself around the word 'Thou'. Was given to hope that my love for God's Name, God's Being and God's Attributes excels my love for any creature, however tender my affection may be towards some on earth and in Heaven.

July 14, 1959

My whole body is full of pain since the beginning of winter. Nothing has helped so far. Lord, give me grace to live with pain and not to murmur. May I learn how to be content in every state. My sleep is broken, and I often feel physically exhausted. But Thy will be done. My sufferings hitherto have been both physical and spiritual. My occasional bodily sufferings have been comparatively easy to bear, but not so my spiritual trials. Sorrow continues to lodge in my heart. God has often been infinitely kind in sweetening the "waters of Marah" through the seasonable application of His precious promises. (*Ex.* 15: 23) Only last night, while I was suffering much, He visited my soul again in the words of Psalm 48, v. 14: "For this God is our God for ever and ever: he will be our guide even unto death". Also Psalm 9, v. 9: "The Lord also will be a refuge for the oppressed, a refuge in times of trouble".

September 24, 1959

Home from Barvas, in Lewis, where I gave assistance at the Communion. The weather was fair, and the attendances large. The Lord brought me through the work, though in much bodily pain and discomfort. Enjoyed a measure of freedom in all the services. Met many dear friends whose kindness was very touching. Mr Donald Morrison, known locally as "Domhnull An Thangaidh", from Eoropie in Lewis, was there; he is like a sheaf of corn ready to be gathered.

October 1, 1959

In private prayer this afternoon I was led to ask the Lord to continue a witness in our family in the coming years as in the past several generations. I should not like this candle to go out. Much affected as I wrestled with the Lord for this great blessing. Afterwards I was much comforted by the 44th Chapter of *Isaiah*, vs. 1-5: "Fear not, O Jacob my servant... I will pour my spirit upon thy seed, and my blessing upon thine offspring... One shall say, I am the Lord's; and another shall subscribe with his hand unto the Lord". May the Day reveal that my request came to the ear of the Eternal. I truly believe it has.

October 10, 1959

The Lord did not chastise me for my late sinful silence at the Throne of Grace. The other evening He drew very near to my soul in the words, "Oh thou my soul, do thou return unto thy quiet rest". (*Ps.* 116: 7)

In Aberdeen I addressed the University Evangelical Union. Though the great majority of our students are out of sympathy with the claims of the Gospel, a good number continue to walk in the old paths. I preached twice on Sabbath. Enjoyed some enlargement in the evening as I commended Christ and His wonderful love to the young.

December 18, 1959

The long and somewhat hurried journey to London has left me very weary. There I preached the quarterly Gaelic sermon in Crown Court Church. There was an excellent congregation, though one felt that a sentimental attachment to the old tongue, Gaelic, drew not a few to the service. In my various journeys through London, I formed the impression that we are moving fast toward many physical sorrows. The Judge is at the door. The ears and the eyes of this generation are so glued to their idols and sins that neither the joyful sound of the Gospel nor the warnings of coming doom reach them. I should not like to live to witness the storms which are coming upon us.

December 23, 1959

Recently I met a young woman in deep spiritual distress. The Lord led me to pray for this soul; and the melting power with which the words of Psalm 30 v. 11 came to my mind, "... thou has put off my sackcloth, and girded me with gladness", I took as a token that God would relieve her in His own time and way. Curiously, I saw this woman in a dream this morning, overjoyed through the singing of these very words. Perhaps in His own mysterious way the Lord has given her rest from trouble through His Word.

1960

January 19, 1960

My recent letters to the *Scotsman*, bearing on the present world situation and our need of repentance in the presence of impending perils, brought the usual crop of letters, both fair and foul. Many fail to see the connection between sin and its punishment. This blindness appears to be greater in the minds of those who profess to be God's ministers; for when they speak, they either follow in the wake of an ungodly world, or just follow their own dim and personal vision.

February 10, 1960

The words of Psalm 139, v. 8, "If I ascend up into heaven, thou art there: if I make my bed in hell, behold thou art there", were again powerfully impressed on my mind. The meaning of these words in their personal application gave me much concern. Yet they have to do with the death of God's believing people whose souls go to Glory, but whose bodies rest in the grave united to Christ until the resurrection; the word 'hell', in its primary signification, means 'the grave'. This thought I found infinitely reassuring and comforting.

February 16, 1960

I was greatly touched in reading in Donald Sage's *Memorabilia Domestica* a reference to the great revival in Lewis over a hundred years ago. He speaks of that favoured Isle as the place "where God is well known and where His Name is truly great". Even now, in a time when spiritual desolation has crept over so many places in the Highlands, Lewis is favoured with God's Presence, and with evidences of His saving power. Some years ago, for example, I met a woman in the Parish of Barvas to whom I apologised outside the Church for prolonging the service. Her answer was, "I could have sat there for ever". How different to the brief and cold formalities one must observe among those to whom God is a stranger, and where His candle is extinguished.

May 7, 1960

An elderly woman tells me that a word of warning I had left her many years ago brought her to her knees to seek salvation. For tokens of mercy such as these, I would thank the Lord.

May 17, 1960

Stood before my bedroom window at dawn. The heavens are a vast cosmic poem declaring the glory of the Lord. The Russians have just launched another space satellite. Man must not only defile this world: he seeks to intrude into a sphere which is not his.[34] When I went back to bed I slept again for a short while. Dreamt that in the melodious voice of my younger days I was singing the first verses of Psalm 23: "The Lord is my shepherd; I shall not want. He maketh me to lie down in green pastures; he leadeth me beside the still waters". The words produced in me the conviction that under the care and guidance of my Father in Heaven I should wait His hour and leading.

June 1, 1960

The meetings of our General Assembly are now over. Listened to a few heated speeches on trifling subjects. Met several dear friends in the Lord. On Sabbath evening I preached in Gaelic in Govan; felt bound and unhappy. "The wind bloweth where it listeth." (*John* 3: 8)

The Church of Scotland has again plunged the country into confusion and the Lord's people into distress through its shocking proposals to destroy the Lord's Day. I could not refrain from tears over this; another blow aimed at Christ's

34 The notion that space satellites trespass on God's realm has a metaphorical slant. Compare the legendary Icarus who perished, not because he made wings and flew, but because he over-reached and flew near the sun. Our vantage-point is enclosed by our horizon, yet in insolent pride (*hubris*) we aspire to God's horizonless view, and are doomed to fall.

crown and glory. A flood of ungodliness is about to overwhelm the land. We can only pray that God may intervene in either mercy or judgement.

June 27, 1960

At Communion in Gairloch, Wester Ross, I was happy to meet a number of the Lord's people. On Sabbath evening I felt much tenderness and melting of soul as I pleaded with the unconcerned to seek the Lord. An old woman afterwards spoke to me in the Manse. Placing her hand over her heart she said with much feeling, "Oh the love of Christ". I spoke to several individuals about the importance of seeking Christ before life's brief day is over.

July 20, 1960

One morning recently I awoke with a comforting word from the lips of my dear Saviour, "...the Lord is with them that uphold my soul". (*Ps.* 54: 4) With this staff in my hand, well may I go forward and engage every foe and face every trial.

September 12, 1960

In Ross-shire we had a visit from Dr Martyn Lloyd-Jones, London. He preached on three successive nights in the Dingwall Free Church; large congregations attended. He has an impressive delivery and a sound Calvinistic doctrine. His love and humility are unfeigned; but his wonted force is now abated through his unremitting labours for Christ and His Cause. His message warmed my heart, which as a result went out in love to the messenger.

September 13, 1960

In reading the Book of *Job*, I was impressed that in his great trials he cursed the night in which he was born. But multitudes of God's suffering people to the end of time will bless God that Job was born and that his trials are recorded in God's word.

This book has been a fountain of comfort to all whom God has chosen in the furnace of affliction. In Chapter 4, he is spoken of as a comforter and friend of God's suffering people. Apart altogether from his own life of holiness, this was one reason why Satan hated him.

November 5, 1960

Winter is now upon us. In the night I felt apprehensive at the thought of another winter in this somewhat isolated corner. After I slept, I dreamt that in a very congenial company I began to sing the words,
"No plague shall near thy dwelling come,
no ill shall thee befall;
For thee to keep in all thy ways
his angels charge he shall." (*Ps.* 91: 10-11)

When I awoke, I knew that the Guardian of Israel had given me another token of His care and love.

November 17, 1960

Home from Glasgow where I conducted Communion services. On Sabbath morning I was astonished at the thoughts which came into my mind as I discoursed on the sufferings of Christ. They came fresh and sweet from the deep well of Truth. These given, spontaneous thoughts seemed to affect some present more deeply. The Holy Spirit enriched the sermon with better thoughts than those I had prepared.

November 26, 1960

This morning I came downstairs early to finish one of my letters to the *Glasgow Herald*. The sad words, "I have sent unto you all my servants the prophets, daily rising up early and sending them" surged into my mind and heart with overwhelming power, and I wept sorely before the Lord. (*Jer.* 7: 25) We seek to speak to a generation who refuse to hear God's Word.

1961

January 7, 1961

Last night I awoke with the words,
"I joy'd when to the house of God,
Go up, they said to me..." (*Ps.* 122: 1)

The thought occurred to me that presently I would be asked to visit some place which would prove to be God's house in truth. Later in the day I had a letter from Mr Murray, in Carloway, Lewis, desiring me to conduct communion services there, where my poor soul often enjoyed a Bethel season.

Our daughter Mary is now engaged to be married to Mr Douglas MacMillan, a student of our church.[35] They seem to love one another deeply. I could only bless them both in the hope that God may make them happy together.

February 9, 1961

A dear friend in the Lord, Mrs Munro, Mount High, Resolis has passed to her everlasting rest. I could not visit her home without being able to say that the Lord was there. Her conversation was invariably on "the things which are above". (*Col.* 3: 1) Her presence in God's house served like a benediction. As one by one of God's dear people go down the valley, one feels as if the darkness is deepening. How sweet is the hope of reunion in the Heavenly Country! Conducted worship in her daughter's home this evening.

Conducted a service in a home in Ferintosh, in the Black Isle. I enjoyed it more than any other since coming to these parts.

35 The Revd James Douglas MacMillan, M.A., minister of Aberdeen Free Church, St Vincent Street Free Church in Glasgow, and Buccleuch and Greyfriars Free Church in Edinburgh. Professor of Church History and Church Principles at the Free Church College (now the Edinburgh Theological Seminary). Previously a shepherd in Argyll (and heavyweight athlete), his most popular book is *The Lord Our Shepherd* (Bryntirion 1983: Evangelical Press of Wales).

Apparently the departed man, a Mr. Gray of Balrainin farm, was a quiet, inoffensive Christian who professed the Lord late in life. An hour of a real sense of God's presence was enjoyed by the Lord's people there.

March 20, 1961

There is in our sinful nature a deep aversion to prayer. A man of God once said that he would rather die than pray. But perhaps our briefest prayers, when shot through with pain, and when arising from the depths of our heart, prevail with God more than our more studied devotions. Two days ago, grieved over the infirmities of my nature, I cried to God several times for the needed grace. That same night I awoke with the precious and reassuring words,
"Thee will I praise, for thou me heard'st,
and hast my safety been." (*Ps.* 118: 21)

April 8, 1961

In the morning yesterday I wondered what subject I should take at the service. My mind was led to the words, "Where is the God of Elijah?" (2 *Kings* 2: 14) I began to think of other memorable days. God gave me His presence and I felt quite tender and melted down in my soul. Enjoyed good freedom all day. In thinking over passages for my next book, I was startled by the words, "God hath anointed thee with the oil of gladness above thy fellows". (*Ps.* 45: 7) May a drop of that anointing with which Christ was blessed fall upon my poor soul. It was an enrichment that went down to "the skirts of his garments", that is, to the whole mystical Body, His Church. (*Ps.* 133: 2)

July 18, 1961

Our summer Communion came to an end last night. The visiting preacher was most touching on the words, "Thou art mine".

The singing on the Thursday evening was unusually sweet and solemn. It remained with me during the whole night. The sweetest hour of all was when I stood before the Lord in the Church hall, less than an hour ago, with the door shut and alone. It was indeed good for me to draw near to God, for He drew near to me. He breathed upon my soul with the warm breath of His mouth, and made me rejoice in the light of His Face. How my heart went out to Him and to all His. He enabled me to pray, especially for the downfall of the kingdom of darkness and the advancement of the cause which is His own.

August 9, 1961

Word reached me that a friend had passed away suddenly. Not long ago I dreamt that we sang together words in Psalm 30, v. 11; "Thou turned hast my sadness to dancing". Afterwards I told him of this 'fellowship'; he was deeply moved. This was my last sight of him on earth.

October 17, 1961

Discussed with friends the various ways in which the Lord communicates His mind to His people. Although some of us differed in the complexion of our personal experiences, we all agreed that God's Word, when it comes in answer to prayer, or in an hour of crisis or trial, ought to be believed. It carries with it a conviction of its own reality and genuineness. It has a corrective or composing effect on the mind. It sanctifies and humbles the soul, and is sweetly appropriate to our state at the time. And it may come in different contexts. It may come within a providential setting, through prayer, or in reading the Word. We may also be sometimes taken by surprise in finding God's Word articulate within our spirit like "a still small voice". (1 *Kings* 19: 12)

October 21, 1961

I have just put the finishing touches to a small book which, God willing, may be of use to our younger people. It is the story of Christ's love to His Bride, the Church, told and illustrated within the typical setting of Rebecca's call and marriage (*Genesis* 24). The title is *The Loveliest Story Ever Told* (Inverness 1962: Highland Printers Ltd), a quotation of Sir Herbert Grierson, the literary critic, who once in my hearing described this chapter as "the loveliest story ever told".

Having finished this task, I did not wish to remain idle during the quiet winter months. Later in the day, as I was out for a walk, a deep desire took possession of my heart that I should now write something which might be of some comfort to God's suffering people.[36]

November 1, 1961

Spent a while in the church hall praying that the Lord might bless me in my labours. The Lord touched my heart and made it tender. In the night I awoke with the words of Psalm 126 v. 12: "My foot standeth in an even place: in the congregations will I bless the Lord". It was a lovely surprise. Today my heart is full of joy. "Thou wilt perform the truth to Jacob, and the mercy to Abraham." (*Micah* 7: 20) May the joy of harvest indeed be mine.

November 8, 1961

With the world situation so much laden with peril for mankind, I felt that I should remember the Lord's people, especially, before Him in prayer. May He cover their head in the day of danger! Felt that I loved dearly all those who love the Lord and who are loved by Him. The words of Ruth, "thy people shall be my people", find their echo in every regenerate heart. (*Ruth* 1: 16) Lord give me greater proof of my love to Thee by bearing the burdens of those who are Thine.

Affected last night by the words of Psalm 46 v. 2-3:
"....we will not be afraid:
Though hills amidst the seas be cast;

36 *In All Their Affliction* by Murdoch Campbell was reprinted several times, most recently in 2003 (Harpenden: Gospel Standard Trust Publications).

Though waters roaring make,
And troubled be, yea, though the hills
by swelling seas do shake."

May His sweet lips so continue to refresh my spirit in the night.

November 25, 1961

Hope I had a taste of "the brooks of honey" as I prayed today in private. (*Job* 20: 17) When the eyes of the soul rest on Christ with desire and delight, God's eyes meet ours; for His eyes also dwell on the same One, the Darling of His bosom, of whom He says, "This is my beloved Son, in whom I am well pleased". (*Mat.* 3: 17)

November 28, 1961

When I awoke this morning, about 5.15, I found the Word of the Lord in my mouth. He is still with me, and I trust I am still with Him. The words were, "Our soul waiteth for the Lord: he is our help and our shield". (*Ps.* 33: 20) I had been greatly harassed in the last several days by fears that the Evil One was spreading a net before my feet. Perhaps he is, but the everlasting arms are, I know, underneath me, and the wings of the eternal over me. Therefore, though I suffer I am safe.

In retiring to bed I was greatly refreshed by a word quoted by my wife from *Ezekiel* 11, v. 16: "...yet I will be to them as a little sanctuary". On the lap of this wonderful assurance I went to sleep in a state of much consolation. The thought of God dwelling with men is an indescribable wonder. In every age and in every place, where even one of His people kneels in prayer, He is there. We may, therefore, under His banner of love, have a little heaven on earth. This afternoon in private the thought of God being 'a little sanctuary' to me was sweet beyond words.

December 11, 1961

Detained by a storm from going outside. I read again the sad story of the theological and constitutional breakdown of the old Free Church. The influences which brought this about were Rainy's passion for 'unity', and his refusal to close the gate against the flood of unbelief - the so-called 'critical' approach to God's Word - under which his own Church has now virtually disappeared.

Rainy was a man of a mesmeric and strong personality, who imposed his own views on a generation of men remarkable for their docility and lack of discernment. All that now remains of his work is a continuance of the spirit of unbelief, along with the same passion for organizational 'unity'. The strife which followed Rainy's work, in our Highlands especially, marked the departure of the blessed spirit of love and peace which made the Disruption Free Church a Bethel on earth. In retrospect, Rainy's work inflicted a great wound on God's cause in our beloved land.

December 14, 1961

This morning I awoke with the words of Psalm 9, v. 14, "That I may show forth all thy praise in the gates of the daughter of Zion". I also felt my spirit very near some of the Lord's people. The words of Psalm 72, v. 15 were also present with me, "And he shall live, and to him shall be given of the gold of Sheba". They are full of comfort because they are full of Christ.

December 20, 1961

The more I read the Psalms the more I agree with the excellent man who once exclaimed, "O, David, however high I rise, you are above me, and however low I descend, you are still beneath me". I question whether any phase of Christian experience is absent from this blessed Book. Its heights touch heaven; its depths touch the very fringe of hell. But, whether we are up or down, He is ever with us.

By the application of Psalm 27, v. 4, I enjoyed, I hope, a taste of Heaven in communion with God: "One thing have I desired of the Lord, that I will seek after; that I may dwell in the house of the Lord all the days of my life".

1962

March 8, 1962

"Draw nigh to God, and he will draw nigh to you." (*James* 4: 8) This is a promise the wonder and truth of which God has just verified in His gracious dealings with my soul. Yesterday I mourned over my remissness in the path of duty; but in the night, the words of Psalm 44, v. 4, "...command deliverances for Jacob", not only awoke me out of sleep, but held my mind and heart throughout the silent watches. These words may have some undisclosed personal application, or they may have to do with the wider sphere of God's cause. But my faith, however feeble at times, has embraced them, and He who sent them shall fulfil them in His own time and way.

March 16, 1962

Communism has swept away the deep defilements which disgraced and morally disfigured so many cities in China. Prostitution, gambling, thieving and irresponsible industrial behaviour, along with the worship of idols, have been swept away by this terrible atheistic scourge. Alas, man's heart is untouched, and no doubt these evils have just gone underground for the time being.[37]

April 9, 1962

While man's physical structure shows that he came out of the dust, on the other hand there are many 'reminders', or evidences, that though now a fallen being, he was created, morally and spiritually, in the image of God. Evolutionary theory concerns nature, and is not designed to explain what transcends nature.[38]

37 In 1962 it was not yet known widely that a political 'scourge' starved, tortured, enslaved and murdered millions of Chinese.

38 Murdo Campbell is not suggesting that theism could be proved by speculative argument, detached from faith. Rather, you *can* doubt that

May 1, 1962

Last night I took upon myself to write an affectionate letter of remonstrance to Dr "Billy" Graham, the American evangelist, who is involved in the so-called Ecumenical Movement.

My beloved wife is away in Aberdeen to see our daughter Mary and her husband Douglas, and I am here alone. More than ever I discover how helpless and lonely one can be without the congenial company of a loved one.

May 12, 1962

The Lord has graciously visited my soul in the words of Psalm 84, vs. 6 and 7. "Who passing through the valley of Baca make it a well... They go from strength to strength." Dreamt that I was singing verse 7, but in a voice and with a power which I cannot now command.

May 30, 1962

Dr Billy Graham has replied to my letter. He is most affectionate, but vague and evasive in his answers to my questions as to where he stands. He is now more at home with the World Council of Churches than with the smaller bodies which keep loyal to the old paths. It is difficult to understand this in a man from whom we expected so much and whose favourite phrase in preaching is, "The Bible says".

June 2, 1962

One persistent plague of my heart is the way vain and unwholesome thoughts flood my poor mind, especially when I lie awake in the night. And yesterday morning the dear Lord rebuked me by awakening me with these words in my mouth,

---

God exists, but given faith – tied to hope and love – you *do* not do so. You have faith similarly in, say, perception: there is no step back from perception which could prove that a red rose 'really' is red. Again, you may correlate one memory with others, your own or other people's, but there is no step back from trust in memory which could let you prove that what you remember happened.

"Fear, and sin not; talk with your heart
on bed, and silent be,
Offerings present of righteousness,
and in the Lord trust ye." (*Ps.* 4: 4-5)

Lord, give me the grace, the power, and such an inward delight in Thy holy Word, as shall enable me to rise above the vanity and corruption of my nature.

Had a visit from a member of a 'Holiness' group who spoke about 'constant victory' and 'the death of the old man'. (*Rom.* 6: 6) He was young, and he believed he had crucified sin and was now perfect. People who speak like this are either deceived, or blessed with a kind of dispositional serenity which one could be misled to substitute for 'perfection'. This claim is contrary to the Word of God and to Christian experience, as it is portrayed or expressed in the lives of God's people from the beginning, both in Scripture and in Christian biography.

Had a letter in the *Scotsman* in defence of the view of the Papal system which we have in the Westminster Confession of Faith. Surprised that my stronger statements were not erased.

June 19, 1962

Back from a Communion at Aultbea, Wester Ross. Apart from the Gaelic 'action' service, I was conscious of much hardness throughout the season. Rev N. MacLeod gave us a vivid and impressive account of the revival in Lewis during which he himself was brought to the Lord.[39] That revival had the spiritual characteristics spoken of in the Book of *Acts*. The proof of its genuineness is to be found in the rich spiritual harvest which followed, and in the constancy of its many converts, some of whom are now "fallen asleep". (1 *Cor.* 15: 18)

We were amused at the 'Grace before Meat' which was once asked by an old man in my native parish in Lewis. The following is a translation.

39 The Revd Norman MacLeod was then Free Church Minister in Portree, Skye, previously in Lochalsh and later in Callanish; father of the Revd Kenneth I. MacLeod, Assistant Minister, Stornoway Free Church.

"Lord, bless the mercies set before us. Bless the young man down in England of whom we hear so much; and her in the red coat. Bless also him who lives in yonder cairn of stones. Amen."

The 'young man' was Spurgeon. The lady in the red coat was Queen Victoria, whose picture he saw on the tea caddy. The man in the 'cairn' was the local proprietor, who occupied the castle in Stornoway.

June 20, 1962

The present persistent argument that the church should freely mix with the world and participate in its ways is full of danger. When a foul stream enters a pure, which is going to suffer? The foul stream contaminates the clean; the clean one does not purify the foul. God's Word is clear and final, "Have no fellowship with the unfruitful works of darkness, but rather reprove them". (*Ephesians* 5: 11)

June 25, 1962

Travelling by plane to North Uist to assist at the Communion in the isle of Grimsay. I was led to speak 'a word in season' to a young friend in the next seat. A similar opportunity presented itself on the return journey, with a young man who was most receptive to my word about the blessedness of knowing Christ as a personal Redeemer. Grimsay is not a pretty isle; but the people there are very kind and affectionate.

July 3, 1962

This afternoon I visited an old man in Resolis who is totally deaf; but he does all the speaking himself. His talk is often worth listening to, for into it he introduces, quite unwittingly, many things which reveal a mind deeply exercised in the things of God. Underneath all the outward 'rudeness of speech' one can see that he has God's Treasure in his heart, and a deep love for God, His Word, His House and His people. (2 *Cor.* 11: 6) Here indeed is a light shining in a dark place, unknown and unseen by men.

Our daughter Mary and her husband rejoice in the gift of a daughter. May she be a 'Lydia' on earth: one whose heart shall ever be open to the Lord and His people. (*Acts* 16: 14)

July 7, 1962

Today and yesterday I mourn over God's silence and His remoteness from my soul.

July 10, 1962

Last night I conversed with a man who left me with the words, 'The morning is coming'. All he meant was that the day was now drawing to its close and that tomorrow would soon be here. But to me the words touched a deeper chord. They reminded me again of the place where there is no night. Afterwards I paced my room and sang the whole of Psalm 130 (to that loveliest of tunes, 'Martyrdom'). The depression and darkness which had shrouded my soul for several days vanished. The Lord was very near. All night, asleep and awake, my mind seemed to dwell on Chapters 53 and 63 in *Isaiah*. The words which were present with me when I awoke were, "For the day of vengeance is in my heart, and the year of my redeemed is come". (*Is*. 63: 4) It looks indeed as if the Lord by "fearful works in righteousness" may soon intervene in His providence and in answer to His people's prayers. The Americans have exploded another bomb of terror: "What shall be the end of these things?" (*Daniel* 12: 8)

August 15, 1962

In Stornoway I was greatly encouraged by the words of Psalm 68, v. 13: "Though ye have lien among the pots, yet shall ye be as the wings of a dove covered with silver, and her feathers with yellow gold". These words made me bow my head and thank the dear Lord.

Travelled home with Rev Robert Sinclair, Wick. He is a most friendly and able man, and his conversation in the train was full of the savour of Christ. He is a staunch Free Presbyterian.

In retrospect, what I enjoyed most of all during this preaching tour was the singing of Psalm 2 in the Stornoway church on Sabbath morning. The singing had that indescribable touch of Eternity which melted my heart and made me feel as if the Holy Spirit brooded over us. It also made me feel how infinitely satisfying is God.

September 3, 1962

Heard Professor John Murray, Westminster, Philadelphia preach on Saturday. He is a solid Calvinist whose books, except for their technical theological vocabulary, are excellent, sound and clear.

September 14, 1962

Repeated my visit to Lewis last week where I assisted at the Kinloch Communion. The weather was favourable and a large congregation was present at each service. There were at least six ministers in the audience on Friday night. Although I missed the tenderness and responsiveness which were present in Skye recently, the Lord did shine upon us, especially while 'serving the Table' on Sabbath afternoon. Something welled up in my heart, and for a moment or two I could not speak. The large number of the Lord's dear people whom I met showed me much affection.

September 18, 1962

Last Sabbath in Lochcarron, Wester Ross, after the evening service, a young minister from Glasgow spoke to me; but I found his conversation most tiring. He spoke about his work in the city where he and his numerous 'teams of helpers gather in the people'. No spiritual qualifications are needed to join the church. Man does everything; God does little or nothing. This is what I inferred from his talk. His attitude to the Sabbath was shockingly lax, and he and good Duncan MacLean, the Church Elder, parted in the heat of argument!

September 24, 1962

This afternoon I was enabled to call on the name of the Lord in private, in the church. I hope He drew my soul after Him, and gave me a season of communion with Himself. An unusual thought came into my mind as I was trying to pray for those who are "the apple of his eye". (*Deuteronomy* 32: 10) I was bold to profess my love to Him since He loved the people I also love. As I thought of Him as the Helper of those who have no help of man, and whose lot here is made up of burdens and tears and grief, I felt a depth of love to Him welling up in my soul. And, I hope, it was when I expressed myself in this way that He bathed my soul in His own love, like a mother whose heart goes out to those who would show kindness to her ailing children. When we love His dear people, we love Himself, and when we truly love Him, we love them.

Felt very depressed during the night because some who listened to me yesterday resented being reminded of their sin. If they would only bow their heads, there might be hope for them.

October 3, 1962

This afternoon and evening I sat down with the Gaelic Bible in the church vestry, and felt deeply affected by the thought that in the great eternity, waves of love from the heart of God will be moving toward the great multitude which no man can number, while the unceasing praises of men and angels shall for ever and ever move, like waves, toward the Throne of God and of the Lamb.

October 18, 1962

Awoke a few nights ago greatly distressed through the powerful application of words from Psalm 116, v. 3 to my mind. "The sorrows of death compassed me, and the pains of hell got hold upon me: I found trouble and sorrow." My only comfort was that this 'trouble and sorrow' was either something which had passed, or the sense of grief which, as I well know, lies persistently in my heart. All day I was wrapped up in a great sorrow. I asked the Lord to comfort and help me. The following night I awoke out of sleep quite melted down, quoting the words of Psalm 3, vs. 7-8: "For thou hast smitten all my enemies upon the cheek bone... Salvation belongeth unto the Lord: thy blessing is upon thy people". God's Word is a "great deep", and it will take eternity to know what lies behind His personal dealings with us. (*Ps.* 36: 6)

October 25, 1962

The present Cuban crisis, so potentially explosive and terrifying, has brought me, like so many others, into a state of anxiety. I suppose that having lived through the two World Wars has left me with latent fears. May I not be spared to see another. The physical and psychological implications of a nuclear war are unknown, but such terror no one could endure. At family worship this evening I read the wonderful words of Elihu: "Where is God my maker, who giveth songs in the night"? (*Job* 35: 10) If only I had the ability to look beyond and above the raging billows which surround us, to Him who reigns and who has promised to keep His own in perfect peace.

November 1, 1962

Slept sweetly last night. Dreamt that I sat beside an old man of a benign and holy face to whom I repeated the words, "He suffered no man to do them wrong: yea, he reproved kings for their sakes; Saying, Touch not mine anointed, and do my prophets no harm". (*Ps.* 105: 14-15) I felt very happy in his company, as if we understood one another and rejoiced in the same great inheritance of God's protection and Word. Perhaps in these days the Lord, who has much people in the world, may restrain the powers which seek to destroy them. May He arise to save all the meek of the earth. Our times are in His hands.

November 16, 1962

Yesterday morning I was much affected by the first verse of Psalm 133: "Behold, how good and how pleasant it is for brethren to dwell together in unity!" Later we happened to have a visit from one of our missionaries in South America, whose conversation concerned the "King of Zion". (*Ps.* 2: 6) His Christian experience touched my own at some points.

November 24, 1962

The marks once said, in Lewis, to distinguish a sincere believer are:
1. Reverence and love for the means of Grace;
2. An open ear to the Word;
3. A kindly eye toward the Lord's people;
4. A liberal hand toward the Cause of Christ; and
5. A heart wholly devoted to Christ in love.
We should covet this set of pearls earnestly before God.

November 26, 1962

Recently I sat beside an elderly woman whose conversation greatly refreshed me. In my prayer I quoted words which moved her to tears. They were words from our Lord's intercessory prayer, "Father, I will that they also whom thou hast given me, be with me where I am". (*John* 17: 24) It happened many years ago that her father was ill, and while she was thinking of him and praying for him, these words took possession of her mind. She was in Glasgow, and her father in the island of Lewis. When these words were whispered in her spirit, she said to someone present, "My father is now with Christ; he has just passed away". Word reached her afterwards that he had passed away at exactly that moment.

December 10, 1962

My recent book, *The Loveliest Story Ever Told*, is having an excellent reception from all evangelical bodies, and the second impression is now being produced. May God bless its message. This is my prayer, as the Lord knows.

December 13, 1962

This morning I awoke with a wistful sense of God's presence in my soul. Also, His Word was in my mouth. This sweet, but all too brief, enjoyment brought back recollections of other days when the secret of God was upon my tabernacle and "When the Almighty was yet with me". (*Job* 29: 5) In those days my mind and heart were not overburdened with the persistent sorrow which lodges there now. Many things contribute to this sorrow, such as the state of God's cause; the blanket of spiritual death which is over the visible Church; lack of Christian fellowship; and the daily warfare with "the body of death". (*Rom.* 7: 24) This morning the Beloved looked for a moment through the lattice of His Word; but now I am alone with the cry within my soul, "Saw ye him whom my soul loveth?" (*Songs* 3: 3)

December 23, 1962

The Lord reminded me that I am remiss in the duty of secret prayer and that through this sin of omission, He might possibly hide His face from my soul. This has produced fear in my heart, and I was led to cry to Him in the night to give me some seal of His love to comfort me. This He did through the words which afterwards awoke me out of sleep, "And they shall be mine, saith the Lord of hosts, in that day when I make up my jewels". (*Malachi* 3: 17) This precious promise He made good to me several years ago, and now He has confirmed it, as He sometimes does, to my poor soul. What a prospect this is, that those who are the special subjects of my prayers shall inhabit the heavenly Canaan.

December 28, 1962

My beloved and precious Saviour gave me a token of His love early this morning in the words of Psalm 103, v. 12: "As far as the east is from the west, so far hath he removed our transgressions from us." O, the infinite merits of Christ's death on the cross through which the sins of His people are forgiven, forgotten, and put away for ever. I suppose in eternity we shall remember our sins; and the knowledge of what it cost God's dear Lamb to redeem us from their power and deserts, shall bind our hearts to Him in an ever-deepening love.

December 31, 1962

For some time now I have been considering writing something on the subject of 'Christian comfort'. This is a difficult and delicate theme. My only qualification for the work is that, in some small measure, I hope I know both what spiritual affliction and God's unfailing comfort are. On Sabbath morning I awoke out of sleep whispering words from the Bible which might indicate the path of duty.

Diminished attendances in the Church did not rob me of a measure of freedom while I preached on the words, "Hitherto hath the Lord helped us". (1 *Sam.* 7: 12) God's sure help comes to his people through His promises, His presence within the soul, and the processes of His holy and wise providence.

1963

January 7, 1963

The old year is gone with all its irrevocable opportunities and deep regrets. May the Lord enable me to 'buy up' life's opportunities in these evil days. Reading the 'death-bed sermons' of a godly French minister whose 'regrets', as he viewed life in retrospect, make solemn reading. Praying that the Lord may deliver me from all unfruitful or unprofitable preoccupation with things of no real value.

The doctrine of 'the second blessing' was the subject of a letter which I had today from an anxious Christian man who feared that, because this blessing has not yet been consciously his, he has no fitness for heaven! No doubt there is a second blessing, as well as a first and a third blessing. We could say that Jacob had a wonderful second blessing, and the apostles on the day of Pentecost. But the rigid modern presentation of this idea is unscriptural and contrary to Christian experience. When God regenerates us He also adopts us, and as an act of grace gives us a right to *all* the privileges of His children. Besides, the Holy Spirit is in our hearts to apply to us the benefits of Christ's redemptive work. No doubt if we are diligent in the way of prayer and enjoying communion with God we get sweet drinks which otherwise would pass us by. The blessings of the believer are not one, or even ten; but are new every morning.

January 20, 1963

In the pulpit today I said a few words on Jabez and his prayer. (1 *Chronicles* 4: 9-10)[40] In a desert of mere names he stands alone like a lovely flower, whose wonderful, if very brief and comprehensive, prayer is its fragrance. The blessing he desired

---

40 "Oh that thou wouldest bless me indeed, and enlarge my coast, and that thine hand might be with me, and that thou wouldest keep me from evil, that it may not grieve me! And God granted him that which he requested."

was God Himself as his everlasting Portion; but since by nature our hearts are too narrow to receive this blessing, he also prays that his 'coasts' might be enlarged. The blessing is there, but we cannot receive it till our hearts are enlarged and opened by the Holy Spirit. The proof of his "newness of life" we find in his desire that God might guide, uphold and preserve him by his mighty hand. (*Rom.* 6: 4) The most spiritual plea of all is that he might be delivered from all evil within and without. May his prayer be also mine.

February 2, 1963

Reading the *Life of Dr Alexander Whyte* by G. F. Barbour. Whenever I read biographical works of Christian ministers I apply three tests, even if they are stringent. I observe how they come in to the Christian life, how they depart this life and, most important, how they behave during their lifetime towards God's cause. In Barbour's *Life* there is no real account of Whyte's spiritual conversion. He died talking about the political situation in India. And his espousal of the modernism of Robertson Smith, as well as his adoration of Cardinal Newman, mark him as a man with little love to God's word or to the witness of the Reformation. His love for Thomas Goodwin and John Bunyan stands in seeming 'contradiction'. We can only hope for the best. The day will declare it. The Church which he opened here in Resolis has disappeared, and all that he said that day about its future had no fulfilment.

February 7, 1963

One of the great evils of my heart is an aversion to continuing instant in prayer, while at the same time I know that there is no joy on earth to be compared with God's 'smile' when we seek His face at the Throne of grace. The other day He drew me towards Him in prayer and gave me sweet tokens of His love. Afterwards I felt my heart going out to God for His unchangeable love for His people, and I felt my heart going out to them for their love to the One whom I also love. I found this outflowing of my heart to Him and to them inconceivably sweet. When I retired to bed He visited me again in the night watches in the words of Psalm 102, v. 20:

"That of the mournful prisoner
the groanings He might hear
To set them free that unto death
by men appointed are."

and from Psalm 4, v. 3: "But know that the Lord hath set apart him that is godly for himself". I hope I could apply these comforting words to some for whom I was praying.

February 15, 1963

Yesterday we laid to rest in the graveyard at Fodderty, Ross-shire, the mortal but precious remains of one of my dearest brothers in the Lord, the Rev Andrew Sutherland, late of Duke Street Free Church, Glasgow. The first time I met this "Israelite indeed" was in Greenock, in 1921 I think. (*John* 1: 47) On that occasion I led the praise for the first time. Since that day we were friends, though separated from each other for long seasons. Throughout the years no cloud or barrier of disagreement came between us. Now that he is gone I feel a blank in my life; but our separation is only for a moment. Many of my dearest friends have crossed the river to the 'Happy Land', and oh, how I long to be with them!

This evening as I was reading a Psalm at family worship I went back, in memory, to the quiet noiseless world of my youth when the only thing we could hear, apart from a passing cart, was the melody of a Psalm at family worship, in almost every home in the community. That world is gone, and the noisy world of violence and 'progress' which is now emerging is moving towards its own terrible end. There are moments when I feel a touch of nostalgia for those quieter days of long ago.

March 5, 1963

At North Tolsta Communion services, in Lewis, I was dispensing the elements and addressing the communicants when the Lord let fall the dew of His grace on our souls. It was a memorable half hour. We tasted the true Bread and the love which is better than wine.[41]

Yesterday I was privileged to meet a choice Christian woman who believed that the Lord would soon call her Home. Before she came to hospital, Christ's words to His bride continued to occupy her mind: "Rise up, my love, my fair one, and come away... the time of the singing of birds is come". (*Songs* 2: 10-12) The words comforted her while, at the same time, they filled her with concern. The solemn prospect of death and eternity can often fill the believer with fear. As I prayed with her the thought came into my mind that the Lord was still to spare her, and that God's word to her soul pointed to new blessings and fresh revivings, which He was to bring out of her trials. Her fear of death and eternity would, I said, seem to show that she is to tarry here for a while yet. When death, at last, would call her away, the love of her Lord would, I believed, dissolve all her fears. She would then long to see Him and to be with Him. The dear woman seemed to think that I was right in my view of her state. I had never seen or heard of her before, and my few minutes at her bedside brought me much consolation and joy of spirit. In the great desert of this world such fragrant lives are rare.

March 19, 1963

My recent season of spiritual deadness the dear Lord was pleased to remove this day. In the night I woke with the Word of the Lord in my mind and mouth; and lest, as sometimes happens, I should forget the precious truths after I had slept

41 You qualify as a communicant member of Murdo Campbell's denomination by demonstrating to the satisfaction of examining Elders your commitment to a Christian life and your desire to remember Christ publicly in the sacrament of Communion.

again, I arose and wrote them down. The word was from the Hundredth Psalm, and was in the form of a command to enter His courts with praise. Later in the day I felt this was a call to the Throne of grace, the inner sanctuary of God's people here. No sooner did I stand before the Lord, alone in the Church Hall, than a wave of His love, and sweet presence, moved over my spirit. Blessed be His Name.

March 28, 1963

A few nights ago I was in a state of fear because the words of Psalm 22, v. 16 filled my mind, "For dogs have compassed me". In the morning I began to prepare the Religion and Morals Report for our Synod; and as I saw how deeply the cause of Christ was menaced by evil men and evil powers, the thought came into my mind that God's word to me "in the night watches" meant that Christ was today suffering in His Cause here. (*Ps.* 63: 6) There are many 'fierce dogs' on the scene who would, if they could, devour and destroy His Cause. Perhaps I also may suffer over some things I mention in this Report. Lord, stand by me if I suffer for the Truth.

Last night I read again a sermon on 'The secret of the Lord' by Dr John Kennedy, of Dingwall Free Church. The experiences on which it touches greatly reassured and comforted me. God does in every age speak to His people in a very intimate and personal, if also secret, way, both by His written Word and in His providence. The God of Israel is not silent to His own, and He with whom there is no 'time barrier' can tell us, if it pleases Him, of things and events which are still hidden in the womb of the future.

Enjoyed a brief hour of Christian communion with a friend at Croy, near Inverness. We saw 'eye to eye' with regard to the different ways in which the Lord converses with His people. The Lord also was present; and I could not but thank Him for this drink from one of His brooks.

April 1, 1963

This morning, my Beloved Redeemer was near to me in the words of Psalm 33, v. 21: "For our heart shall rejoice in him, because we have trusted in his holy name". Later in the day a wave of joy passed over my soul as I reflected on all that is involved in His Name, and how each name He bears is so sweetly related to my needs and state. His name is a spiritual treasure-house, inexhaustible and glorious.

April 22, 1963

On Wednesday I listened to Dr Martyn Lloyd-Jones preaching in Inverness. His evening sermon ended on a note of longing to be with Christ. My love went out to this dear man in a way that I cannot describe.

May 1, 1963

Reading an article on the recent Pentecostal Movement within some of the rigid and very ritualistic Episcopal Churches in America. Those who are affected by this movement claim that they have undergone a spiritual conversion, and that the Bible is now 'a living Book' to them. Dr Lloyd-Jones said recently that God's spirit is at work among such bodies, but that while life was there, there was, on the other hand, great need of guidance and direction along sober and Scriptural lines. They were like children who, if left to themselves, do wrong things and say wrong things; but they live and have spiritual zeal and vitality! The Church in Corinth was made up, he said, of such children in Christ. May God indeed open our graves, and may those who emerge out of darkness be led to order their lives according to God's word. Life, even when its movements are uneven, is infinitely better than death. Pentecostalism, however, is in many ways dangerous and unbalanced.

May 11, 1963

On Thursday evening at our local Prayer Meeting the Lord refreshed my spirit when I spoke of "the waters of Marah" which He sweetened for His people by casting in a tree, which miraculously rendered the embittered waters pleasant and wholesome. (*Ex.* 15: 23) The whole subject opened up before me so that when I spoke about how the Cross of Christ, the Love of Christ, His Promise and "a good hope through grace" can sweeten life's trials, a few eyes began to fill with tears. Others enjoyed the blessing which I enjoyed myself. My poor soul needed this unexpected feast. After I retired to sleep God gave me another blessing through the words of Psalm 31, v. 19: "Oh, how great is thy goodness, which thou hast laid up for them that fear thee; which thou hast wrought for them that trust in thee before the sons of men!"

May 15, 1963

Had a wonderful moment of deep communion with the Lord as I walked on the Newmills road in Resolis last night. My heart panted after the Lord. My soul felt like a caged bird which longed for its release from the bondage of this mortal and sinful life, and for the enjoyment of uninterrupted fellowship with Christ where my Sun "shall no more go down". (*Is.* 60: 20) It is good to think that He has created no desire in the soul which he will not 'accomplish' and satisfy. And the deeper the thirst the more satisfying shall be the drink!

June 8, 1963

Last night as I walked again on the Newmills road my heart was greatly touched and melted down through the powerful application of the words of Psalm 78, v. 6: "That the generation to come might know them [his testimony and his law], even the children which should be born; who should arise and declare them to their children". As I watched some passing by to attend the local dance, with all its dangerous associations, I prayed earnestly for the day when the young might be won for Christ, and especially for those who are yet unborn, that God might rescue them from the destructive habits of this age. In the church vestry, alone, I could only sob, out of a broken heart, my desire and prayer. The Lord, I hope, was near, as I prayed that He might once more pluck His hand out of His bosom to save us. The gracious sign which He afterwards gave me that He was present was most impressive. The thought also came into my mind that since the hour was spiritually so late and so dark, we should initiate something like praying groups here and there. Lord, lead me in the right path. But how can we pray if the spirit of prayer and watchfulness is denied?

June 17, 1963

The plague of my heart is a perpetual source of grief to me. In the night, when sleep eludes my eyes, I try to arrest or direct the foolish and sinful thoughts which invade my mind. When I cannot get my mind to rest on the Word, I try other ways of escaping from the grievous law of sin and from all carnal thoughts. I try to count all the flowers, trees, birds, beasts and fishes I know. This harmless, if unprofitable, mental exercise is a mere diversion to get away from the evil heart which only God can cure. The words of the Psalmist describe my state:
"For a disease that loathsome is
so fills my loins with pain..." (*Ps.* 38: 7)

On the other hand, all my desire is before the Great Physician. It is that He might make me whole. And while the soul is in the grip of sin, my poor body is often weak. Sensations of great infirmity often creep in upon me. He who knows our frame and who remembers that we are dust came very near to me in the words, "The Lord will strengthen him upon the bed of languishing: thou wilt make all his bed in his sickness". (*Ps.* 41: 3)

June 19, 1963

Very early this morning the Lord visited me in the words of Psalm 18, v. 28: "For thou wilt light my candle: the Lord my God will enlighten my darkness". These words, precious beyond a thousand worlds, I sang in my sleep. When I awoke His presence and love filled my soul. He also composed my mind, for I had been perplexed as to how to apply certain passages of His Word, which had been present with me for several days. His Word is "a great deep", and the manner and nature of its fulfilment only His Providence here, and Eternity afterwards, can perfectly reveal.

But our life here is made up of sunshine and clouds, of night and day. Certain words from Psalm 22 remind me that if I serve the Lord I must share in the fellowship of His sufferings, and be put in the likeness of His death. We must drink of the cup which He drank of, and come under the baptism of fire and persecution here. Lord, I need Thy upholding grace.

This morning I had a lovely dream. I dreamt that I entered a small room where a company was singing Psalm 133. When I entered, the one who led the singing pointed to the last verse, verse 3, and asked me to sing it. A lovely ray of golden light rested on the words as I began to sing them.

"As Hermon's dew, the dew that doth
On Sion' hills descend;
For there the blessing God commands,
Life that shall never end."

I awoke much awed and refreshed by the Presence of Him Who had sealed His Word on my spirit. As I always do, I dismissed the dream, but embraced the unfading treasure, God's Word of promise.

Read this morning at Family worship the passage in *Hebrews* which speaks of the hope of the true Church of God as an anchor of the soul which is "both sure and steadfast". (*Heb.* 6: 19) Christ, the invisible Rock of Ages, is the source and secret of this steadfastness. In Him our hope is fixed. Adam, our first covenant head, had his anchor fixed on his own righteousness, a mere movable stone which proved utterly inadequate when the force of Hell's temptation bore down on the poor bark which carried not only himself, but all humanity in him. If God had not led him to the Rock against which 'the gates of hell cannot prevail', the force and terror of his sin, and of God's wrath, would have swept him and us down to perdition. (*Mat.* 16: 18) There is no folly that can be compared to the folly of those who imagine, as foolish sinners do, that their own dead hope, fixed to their own righteousness, which is rejected by God, can stand up to the terrors of death and God's judgment.

July 10, 1963

On a pastoral visit to a home where I can always breathe, spiritually speaking; for the conversation is in Heaven. After another visit, I left the dear man I called on in tears as he mentioned the NAME which, to all who love the Lord, is an ointment poured forth. His next-door neighbour is dying, but the strange unwelcoming look that came over her face as I spoke to her made me leave the room.

August 29, 1963

On the island of Lewis, I called at Ness and took a walk to the seashore where I spent so much of my boyhood. Was much affected by the recollection of a wonderful and vivid dream I once had then of meeting the Lord Jesus on that lovely shore. I still remember His kiss of welcome as I joined His friends who stood by His side. I also recall his words.

September 4, 1963

For several weeks now God has been remote and silent to me. This is what I dread; but I was silent also, and remiss in secret prayer. Two evenings ago, however, I spent a while alone in the church building, where I felt I had access into His blissful presence. His love touched my heart and melted me down. In the night He refreshed my spirit in the words of Psalm 34, v. 19, "Many are the afflictions of the righteous: but the Lord delivereth him out of them all". May I be enabled to keep near to Him, and to overcome my neglect of secret prayer.

September 8, 1963

The recent death of the Rev Ranald Fraser, late of Lochcarron Free Church, Wester Ross, has touched me deeply. He was a man of God, and one who enjoyed great nearness to the Lord in prayer. His devotional life was almost continuous; while his delight in singing psalms and spiritual songs made his company very pleasant. I saw him lying on his couch a few days before he died. I whispered to him the words of Psalm 18, v. 28: "For thou wilt light my candle: the Lord my God will enlighten my darkness". I kissed him a fond 'farewell' till we meet again 'in sweet Jerusalem'.

Few of God's people are able, in the article of death, to say anything of what they apprehend and enjoy as they stand on the threshold of the Eternal World. The earthly Tabernacle is about to dissolve; but in any case, the soul has taken a forward leap into the dimension of eternity. Therefore to speak of what we see and enjoy becomes a spiritual impossibility. In the opposite direction the same holds true of the ungodly. The terrors which loom before them render them incapable of expression. But some in both camps *have* spoken of their apprehensions, so that "at the mouth of two witnesses, or three witnesses" the awesome prospect of a blissful or a hopeless eternity is established. (*Deut.* 17: 6) In prayer after considering this I could not but thank God for a good hope through grace, and for being the God He is from everlasting to everlasting.

October 15, 1963

My sister Mary, in the isle of Harris, has forwarded me a 'grace before meat' by a quaint local Christian.[42] Here it is. "Lord, bless the people of Lewis and Harris. They had a church down at the shore where they used to pray when I was a boy. And when I was at sea we had, as Thou knowest, a bo'sun called Neil, and when the hour would be dark and stormy Neil would keep saying, 'She'll go through; she'll go through.' That is how we are, Lord, when the Black Fellow chases us; but we'll get through in spite of him; for Jesus' sake, Amen."

This grace was not borrowed, but came straight from the heart!

November 7, 1963

In Inverness at a meeting I heard an energetic little woman who had laboured in China for many years. She spoke for over an hour. Her appeals were very sincere, but nothing touched me. One could only admire her courage and sacrifices, as well as her devotion to the Lord.

Called on the Rev Kenneth MacRae, minister of Stornoway Free Church, who is ill in the Infirmary. Felt the Lord's presence as I prayed by his bedside. A faithful soldier of Jesus Christ is about to lay down his armour. He is weary from his journey, and needs the rest which remains for the people of God.

Tonight I preached to a respectably-sized congregation at our Harvest Thanksgiving service, in this farming community, from the words of Psalm 68, v. 10. "Thy congregation hath dwelt therein: thou, O God, hast prepared of thy goodness for the poor." Reminded the people to be rich toward God and in knowledge of the real blessings of the Gospel. "O earth, earth, earth, hear the word of the Lord." (*Jer.* 22: 29)

---

42 Murdo Campbell's elder sister Mary married the kind, gentlemanly John MacLeod, teacher and lay missionary on St Kilda from 1926 to 1929. One photograph, often reproduced, shows him with ten of his pupils in 1927.

November 14, 1963

Reading an excellent little book by Agnes Beaufort, who was a member of John Bunyan's congregation at Bedford. The book was apparently transcribed from her own manuscript in the British Museum. It is the story of one whom this world hated because of her devotion to the Lord, to His work and His servant. Christian love between God's people is something which Satan has always tried to misrepresent and to give another name. God's vindication is often terrible; and the enemies of this lovely young woman were at last seen in their true colours as the emissaries of "the accuser of the brethren".

November 22, 1963

During my customary walk around Newmills, Resolis, I was favoured with the Lord's presence; He truly warmed by heart with His love. Felt an hunger and a panting of spirit after Him, and a longing for the day when I shall see Him as He is, not through a glass darkly, but face to face. Yesterday morning I awoke greatly refreshed by the words of Psalm 107, v. 9: "For he satisfieth the longing soul, and filleth the hungry soul with goodness". This is His promise. My thirst anticipates the drink, and my spiritual hunger the feast which shall satisfy my soul.

The wireless, at the moment, is giving out the news that President John F. Kennedy of America has been shot dead in Texas. God's providence is unpredictable, and our restless world is in terror and confusion.

December 7, 1963

Last night my wife drew my attention to a sentence in Donald Sage's *Memorabilia Domestica* about the decline of vital godliness in the Black Isle which, he says, began after the death of Mr Calder, minister of Ferintosh Free Church. There were times when his successor, Dr John MacDonald, in passing from the south to the far north of the country, would refuse to visit his own parish. Mr Sage seems to think that these long absences from his parish brought about this spiritual decline; but my opinion is that Dr MacDonald was already aware that God's candlestick had been removed, and that he preferred to labour where the Spirit had not yet been grieved away. And the decline has continued through these long, long years. When will God turn His feet to these long desolations?

December 9, 1963

Reading again one of my favourite bedside books, the *Thoughts* of Blaise Pascal.

1964

January 11, 1964

In Lewis a dear friend, Mr John MacLeod, Cross, known as 'the Professor' during my schooldays, gave me recordings of his voice leading a congregation in praise. They are Gaelic psalms sung in the traditional style. Mr MacLeod is a member in the Church of Scotland, and I was deeply affected by his singing of 'Walsall' and 'Montrose'. Nothing touches my spirit more than the dear Psalms of David, properly sung. The Lord has often, I hope, led me, warned me, and comforted me by means of those Songs of Zion.

January 31, 1964

My Beloved Lord, who is also my Friend, visited my soul in the night watches. I dreamt that I was walking under a calm and lovely sky and, at the same time, singing the eleventh verse of Psalm 30. "Thou hast turned for me my mourning into dancing: thou hast put off my sackcloth, and girded me with gladness." Awoke in a state of great consolation. The day will come when the Lord shall divest me of the garments of sorrow, and when the night of weeping shall be turned into a morning of joy.

February 10, 1964

Was refreshed and reassured in reading again a sermon by Dr John Kennedy, Dingwall, Ross-shire on 'Communion with God'. The subject is difficult, since its personal nature brings it into a dimension not known to every species of religion. But God is personal, and holds communion with His people in every age. He is not silent to them. If we are His companions in the way of life He gives us intimations of His mind and purpose in relation to ourselves, our loved ones, His providence and His cause. My own difficulty is whether I ought to reveal His disclosures of His mind to me in relation to the future. Man's 'unbelief' would not accept these things; and to me, perhaps they are too terrible to relate wholly.

March 1, 1964

Truly "it is not good for man to be alone"! (*Gen.* 2: 18) Since a week now I have occupied the manse in Resolis in the silence of utter solitariness. My beloved wife, whose gentle voice and lovely face always make the home a pleasant place to live in, is in Edinburgh with our daughter Mary.

March 23, 1964

Mourning over an old plague of my heart, a neglect of duty at the Throne of grace. Often, when the thought comes into my mind that I should go aside to pray, all kinds of 'urgent' matters obtrude themselves on my attention. As one of the Puritan Fathers says, there is at times in our heart a deep aversion to prayer. This is what Satan plays on and uses to our spiritual detriment. Even the unspeakable joys of God's presence, and God's answers which reach us through prayer, fail to cure this wretched disinclination to "call upon the name of the Lord". (*Ps.* 116: 17)

March 28,1964

Felt a little encouraged this morning when I thought of God's people in other days, and that in their loneliness they enjoyed secret communion with the Lord in His House. It was thus with Anna and Simeon. The formal services of the temple were without life, and not graced by the spiritual presence of the Lord; but He was with the "two or three" who waited on Him in secret. (*Mat.* 18: 20) In the church alone this morning I found this thought a great comfort, for this is how I am also. Our public services seem to be just formal, while "drops from heaven" fall on my spirit in secret. On Thursday at our Prayer meeting I tried to speak of the causes of the Lord's absence in our public gatherings, but it will take more than man's voice to stir those who lie on the lap of unconcern.

April 12, 1964

The other evening, motoring alone over Mount Eagle, Resolis I was much refreshed in my soul by the words of Psalm 5, v. 7, "But as for me, I will come into thy house in the multitude of thy mercy: and in thy fear will I worship toward thy holy temple". The thought of appearing before God in Heaven melted me down. And we need a 'multitude of mercy' to sustain and preserve us on the way there. It is by grace that we reach glory. I longed for the day when I would be able to praise and love Him as I desire. His own people will come to Him through endless ages with sacrifices of praise.

April 16, 1964

After three homes in our congregation had been desolated by death I was constrained, on two Sabbaths in succession, to mention that two other homes would be shut very soon. It then transpired which homes were meant. The Lord, in His own way, placed this burden on my spirit. If only those who remain, and especially those who are coming near the end of their journey here, would heed these warnings!

Last night, with my body asleep but my heart awake, I seemed to enjoy fresh and glorious views of the Lord Jesus as the God-Man who, in His humiliation and exaltation, conquered death, abolished sin, and is now crowned with many crowns. Truly my sleep was sweet to me. When I awoke I found these words in my mouth, "I will now turn aside, and see this great sight". (*Ex.* 3: 3) Before I went to bed I was greatly refreshed by a spiritual song composed by James MacMillan of Kilchoan, Argyll, the father of my son-in-law Douglas MacMillan.

May 10, 1964

Arrived home yesterday after attending the funeral of the Rev Kenneth MacRae, Stornoway. He was a 'Mr Valiant for Truth' in His day. As a preacher he was simple, clear and brief, while he could wield a powerful and sharp sword in his constant warfare against the enemies of God's word, and of the Reformed witness. Transparent and simple as a child, he was as bold as a lion in the cause of Righteousness. May the Lord raise up others who shall stand in the breach in a dark day.

June 21, 1964

At Kinlochewe, Wester Ross, I visited the brook where, fourteen years ago, I pleaded with the Lord to give me grace to overcome my infirmities, especially my restlessness of spirit. Felt quite overcome as I remembered the many clouds which came between my soul and Christ since that day; but I was able to thank Him for the needed daily grace so faithfully bestowed.

A person with whom I conversed on the subject of faith in Christ seemed to value the word of exhortation. As a token, I hope, that He blessed my words, His sweet and solemn presence tarried with me for a while, after I retired to my bedroom.

Awoke a few mornings ago with words which made me believe that another dear friend in the Lord had died. And last night I was told that a friend had passed away. This excellent girl was an ornament of grace.

July 6, 1964

When I awoke in the middle of the night God's word was present with me. It came as a reminder that as the world hated Him it also hates all who are truly His. This hatred is not confined to 'the world' as such, but often we see it working through some within the visible Church. Oh Lord, save me from harbouring such a spirit against any on earth. By Thine own love in my heart may I be enabled to love my enemies, and to pray for their eternal welfare.

Only for these welcome visits from Christ, the Physician and Shepherd of my soul, how lonely and bleak my life here would be. When He comes to me, a poor patient in His hospital, His voice and smile are a balm to my broken spirit, and manna from Heaven. Without this portion from time to time I mourn.

July 14, 1964

This morning I awoke with the sweet Name of the Beloved in my mouth. Felt my soul embracing Him; but the painful distractions of life, and my persistent sinfulness of heart, soon left me mourning over His absence.

July 16, 1964

For several terrible years a great fear lodged in my heart that I had committed an unpardonable sin; but in front of the Cross on which God's 'dear Lamb' endured and bore all my woes, and the curse which they deserved, I saw His glory and merits rising infinitely beyond them all. The figures which the Bible uses to portray this fact melted my heart and filled me with awe and wonder. "I will now turn aside and see this great sight." (*Ex.* 3: 3) "For as the heaven is high above the earth, so great is His mercy toward them that fear Him." (*Ps.* 103: 11) "Thy mercy, Lord, is in the heavens; and thy faithfulness reacheth unto the clouds." (*Ps.* 36: 5) But eternal ages cannot exhaust this wonder. No sinner who looks to Christ in the merits of His death need despair, though in his fear of his sins, he might, like Heman, be laid "in the lowest pit". (*Ps.* 88: 6)

July 29, 1964

For several days I have been affected by the thought that should God at last welcome me into His holy presence I would spend Eternity before Him with my head bowed at the wonder of such a sinner being there. I believe that just as our knowledge of God, and our love to Him, shall continue to deepen throughout Eternity, so shall our holy humility do so also. "God is greatly to be feared in the assembly of the saints, and to be had in reverence of all them that are about him." (*Ps.* 89: 7) Ah, Lord prepare me, and deliver me from the plague of my heart.

July 31, 1964

When I retired to bed, sin and Satan seemed to come into my soul like a flood. The Lord rebuked me by His Word for not resisting the adversary more steadfastly. The cry of another was wrung from my trembling heart, "O wretched man that I am! who shall deliver me from this body of death?" (*Rom.* 7: 24) Lord, be merciful to me a sinner.

August 1, 1964

After the fears and the conflicts of the previous day the Lord was pleased to comfort me in the night. When at last sleep touched my eyes I had a dream that I began to address a holy-looking company on the words, "But unto you that fear my name shall the sun of righteousness arise with healing in his wings". (*Mal.* 4: 2) Awoke greatly comforted and much relieved that the blessed One, against whom I so often sin, is still my Comforter and Friend.

September 13, 1964

This morning I awoke with a prayer on my lips that the Lord would hasten the day when His glory would fill the whole earth.

October 12, 1964

For the last several mornings I have been reading the *Epistle to the Ephesians*. The many deep and clear insights into the heart and mind of God which are given in this Epistle are astonishing. We are brought to see the love of Christ which passeth knowledge, like an ocean without a shore, and fathomless. It is a love ever flowing towards His Church, that is, His people. And it never ebbs. These disclosures are not something which we just "apprehend" as a matter of objective revelation. Of this fullness the Church of the 'first-born' drink. Also, the river of grace, which makes glad God's city, flows into the hearts of all whom He has quickened by His Spirit.

Again, though they thirst and hunger here, water from the Rock follows them and their bread is given daily from Heaven. But, as this Epistle reveals, we are here only touching the fringe of the unending pleasures which are for evermore at God's right hand.

October 20, 1964

Last night after my return from the Communion at Olrig, in Caithness, I retired to rest in much weariness and under a great burden of depression. But the Lord comforted my soul in a wonderful way. In a dream I found myself sitting beside a beautiful and holy person who, with indescribable sympathy and tenderness, quoted the words of Isaiah 63, v. 9: "In all their affliction He was afflicted, and the angel of his presence saved them". Such a voice I seldom, if ever, heard in this world. It was full of holy pathos and love, showing that He who was a man of sorrows here is still touched with a feeling of our infirmity. Help me, dear Lord, to remember this night whenever I am crushed and bowed down under my burdens. Give me resignation, knowing that my light affliction is for but a moment.

October 25, 1964

Last night I felt a great peace taking possession of my heart; and in the early morning I was greatly comforted and reassured by God's word that I still have a place in the prayers of some of God's people who, I feared, had forgotten me: "Behold, how good and how pleasant it is for brethren to dwell together in unity!" (*Ps.* 133: 1)

November 14, 1964

Enjoyed a visit to a Communion in North Uist, despite my earlier fears. Felt it easy to speak to the people there. The weather was ideal. I seldom saw a fairer scene than the Cuillin and Wester Ross hills as I journeyed home by boat and car. Nature was bathed in the warm mellow sunshine of late autumn.

My conversation with two young friends, on the urgent need of seeking the Lord in a day of grace, warmed my own heart; and I hope the word did not fall on fallow ground.

The Rev Mr Philip, the Church of Scotland Minister at Holyrood in Edinburgh, gave a lecture to the Graduates' Fellowship in Inverness which I much enjoyed. It was on the 'imperatives' of God's moral law. The address would really have done credit to Charles Hodge.[43] Such men are, at the moment, greatly needed in a Church whose ministry is largely following its own dreams.

November 21, 1964

Reading of a Godless but wealthy man who, in his illness, wrote a friend about his impending death. 'I lie awake at night to hear the worms in the churchyard sharpening their claws for me.' What a contrast between these words and those of a poor, but gracious, man who said a few hours before he died, 'I am listening to the redeemed in glory as they sing the Song of Moses and of the Lamb.' Between these two attitudes of spirit there is a great gulf fixed which shall remain unspanned throughout Eternity.

November 30, 1964

Yesterday I preached on the parable of the ten virgins. I found particularly solemn the words of the Lord in refusing to open the door to the foolish ones. "I know you not." (*Mat.* 25: 12) There is a way in which He who knows all things knew them also. But these voices crying to Him from behind the shut door were utterly strange to Him. They were not the voice of His dove, or of His children. He knows the voice of His people who cry to Him out of a broken heart and out of a sense of need. Here on earth God is in communion with His own. He speaks to them and they talk and walk with Him. All other voices are strange in

---

43 Charles Hodge was Professor of Theology at Princeton Seminary, U.S.A., from 1822 to 1878. His three-volume *Systematic Theology* (1872-73) was the standard text-book for generations of Free Church ministers.

His ears. This loving and mutual converse between Christ and His flock would make it impossible for Him to address these words to any of His. The implication of knowing Christ's voice is that, in a deeper and truer sense, He knows ours. Therefore a welcome awaits us, and an open door into His presence.

December 13, 1964

In Maryburgh, Ross-shire, I had the pleasure of listening to my dear friend, the Rev Alexander MacLeod, of Nairn. He was my beloved companion and neighbour in Glasgow for fourteen years. His sermon was based on the words, "Then Samuel took a stone and set it ...and called the name of it Ebenezer, saying, Hitherto hath the Lord helped us". (1 *Sam.* 7: 12) Later, as we sat together in the manse, we spoke of this sweet word as embracing the present and future life of the believer. He will be our guide and help till we pass the last dark stream. There he shall be with us also, to lead us safely into the rest and joy of Heaven. The sermon possessed the flavour of other days when we used to enjoy God's presence in the means of grace in our beloved Glasgow congregations. My dear friend is pining for the heavenly Canaan.

This evening as I was thinking of the glorified Church in Heaven I was again impressed by the truth that those who make up the multitude of the redeemed belong to every nation and tribe. Heaven is a place where all racial distinctions are unknown. Black, white and yellow shall be there. True Christians should not quarrel over the colour of one's skin, for this is offensive to God. Moses married a woman of Ethiopia, and those members of his family who found fault with him in this matter were severely reprimanded by God. God's people shall love one another everlastingly in Christ, for they are all one in Christ Jesus.

December 17, 1964

This morning I was refreshed by the words of Psalm 148, v. 14, "...the children of Israel, a people near unto Him". Throughout the day I was exercised in my mind over these great words. The spiritual Israel of God are near to Him in covenant bonds and in an eternal relationship of love and righteousness. "Thy Maker is thy husband." (*Is.* 54: 5) There is also a nearness of nature. He has their nature, and they partake of His. He has graven them on the palms of His hands, and the decree of election, redemption, and glorification shall bring them into His presence where they shall see Him as He is. But this sea is too vast to describe. Eternity cannot exhaust the bliss inherent in the words, "near unto Him".

1965

January 6, 1965

The nervous strain from which I am suffering at the moment has constrained me to call more earnestly on the name of the Lord for the needed strength to endure it. And last night He visited my soul through the words of Psalm 93, v. 4:
"But yet the Lord, that is on high,
is more of might by far
Than noise of many waters is, or great sea-billows are."
I thank God for this measure of relief.

January 23, 1965

In the early morning I was arrested by these words of Psalm 147, v. 3: "He healeth the broken in heart, and bindeth up their wounds".

I was soon to discover that God's promise had a spiritual meaning; for Satan, as he so often does, began to throw his "fiery darts" into my soul. (*Eph.* 6: 16) And how deep are those wounds which I carry in my soul through his fearful and often blasphemous temptations. There is no limit to his wickedness, though there is, thank God, to his power. My greatest grief comes through the fact that his temptations so often reflect on the glory, holiness, perfection and truth of Him against whom - if I had the power to do so - I would rather die than sin. I suppose many of God's dear people are often in such depths - each thinking that his own, or her own, sin is more evil than any other. The prospect of death is sweet if it means eternal separation from sin and Satan. To many the wonder of God's forgiveness is something which shall deepen within their souls throughout eternity. Often have I felt that my sins of thought and imagination were unpardonable; but I look to the blood of the Lamb of God, and to the mercy of Him, which through His merits, rises infinitely beyond our greatest sins. Let me ever carry the prayer of another in my heart, "God be merciful to me a sinner". (*Luke* 18: 13)

February 17, 1965

Yesterday I met a man in Dingwall, Ross-shire who told me about two men who each witnessed on the side of the Lord. The one in 'speaking to the Question' ended his remarks by saying that whatever bitter herbs God's people might have to taste of in this life there was one herb which would always remain sweet. Then he quoted the words, "Jesus Christ, the same yesterday, today and forever". (*Heb.* 13: 8) How true and how full of consolation are such words. The other man was on his death bed, and on being asked by those who stood by if he was leaving anything behind him, he said, "To you I am leaving Hope and Faith; but I am taking Love with me".

Had a letter from the widow of the dear and godly Professor A. M. Renwick, who is now clothed with the Sun in glory. He died suddenly. He was truly a prince and a great man in Israel. May I be ready also when Death shall knock at my door. Enable me to watch and pray, O Lord.

April 17, 1965

My dear and much beloved friend, the Rev Alex. MacLeod, minister of Nairn Free Church, has passed away suddenly while visiting the Holy Land. His deep piety and gentlemanly bearing could not but impress those who knew him intimately. One after another of my friends are being called away. "Be ye also ready." (*Mat.* 24: 44) Shortly before he passed away, and as he was crossing the river Jordan on a bus, he said to a friend that it would be good if their crossing of the last river of death would be as easy as crossing the literal river. We believe it was so for him.

May 30, 1965

Retired to my secret place in our church hall a few evenings ago to find the Lord there "waiting to be gracious". (*Is.* 30: 18) I had been apprehensive that my neglect of these secret and spiritual duties would draw forth the chastisement of His withholding His ear from my plea, and His presence from my soul. Instead He was easily entreated. May He continue to show Himself "through the lattice", and may I continue to call upon His name. (*Songs* 2: 9) In the night I awoke with the words, "Thou didst confirm (or refresh) thine inheritance, when it was weary". (*Ps.* 68: 9) Without these 'drops from Heaven' I would faint in the way. Christ's mouth is indeed sweet when from His very lips He gives the needed grace without which we cannot live, spiritually speaking.

July 9, 1965

This morning I was again deeply touched by the miracle of the dry bones coming to life through the invocations of the prophet. There are times when the Church of God looks as if it had perished, but how glorious and astonishing is God's power in giving her an instant resurrection and clothing her with power! In the very hour when her enemies rejoice over her decay, powerlessness and death she springs to life, "terrible as an army with banners". (*Songs* 6: 10) God laughs at the efforts of a Godless world, and of her great adversary, to keep her in her grave. So do we. The same power, of "exceeding greatness", which brought Christ out of the grave is the power which works in all who believe. This thought affected my soul so much that I had to go at once to my usual corner in the church hall, where I sobbed out my cry that He might arise and plead the Cause which is His own.

August 1, 1965

I recently visited in hospital a Miss MacQueen from Moy, Inverness. As I engaged in prayer I felt, as I sometimes do when I pray with the Lord's people, something which I find difficult to describe touching my heart and mind. It is like a 'sensation' of peace and holiness, as if the person for whom I pray dwelt in God's very presence. I had never seen this benign-looking woman before. Her face radiated the peace which "passeth all understanding". (*Philippians* 4: 7)

The Rev Walter MacQuarrie, minister at Knockbain in the Black Isle, has passed to his eternal rest and reward. Physically a very strong man, his sermons were preached with an impressive emphasis. He was a forceful, lucid, expository preacher, and if at times somewhat abrupt and difficult in Church Courts he was, on the other hand, a man to be admired for the consistency of his walk. He laboured for over forty years in Knockbain.

Felt greatly refreshed yesterday by the last verse in Psalm 23: "Surely goodness and mercy shall follow me all the days of my life: and I will dwell in the house of the Lord forever". The Comforter of Zion, I hope, gave me this much needed drink from the well of Truth at a time when I felt weary in the way.

August 10, 1965

At the Portree communion, in Skye. Heard a friend speak of the joy of having God's presence restored to his soul. Listened to a young woman from Lewis singing a most spiritual Gaelic song on the faithfulness of Christ as the Chief Shepherd of His flock. Motoring to Broadford, I felt also the deep calm of the Cuillin hills, with a full yellow moon showing its face now and again between the peaks as we passed. And a sweet sense of the Lord's nearness tarried with me during the solemn season.

August 24, 1965

On a walk on the Balblair road in Resolis, I hope the Lord was my companion. Sang and repeated the whole of Psalm 72, which has a spiritual and literary beauty beyond compare. The various natural figures used by the Holy Spirit to describe the rule, the grace, the kingdom and the great peace awaiting our world during the glory of the latter days affected me deeply. In that day "the shout of a king" will be among the nations of the earth as they join in their songs to Him who is their Desire and through whom and by whom they shall be blessed. (*Numbers* 23: 21)

Heard that a minister friend awoke out of a long and deep coma a little before he died. "Am I still here?" he asked, with a sad look. "I was in heaven for a while." Shortly afterwards he breathed his last. He was a man I loved deeply.

October 12, 1965

On the way home from Lochcarron, Wester Ross, my heart was touched by the words, "Abide with us, for it is toward evening and the day is far spent". (*Luke* 24: 29) My sun is declining towards setting, but the conscious presence of my Saviour would make the evening of my days a prelude to an eternal morning.

Was deeply affected by the death of a Miss Macleod of Raanish, in Lewis, whose conversion happened through my twice quoting portions of God's word to her. My soul was bound to her ever since in the love of Christ, and one of my regrets is that I did not get to know her better.

November 12, 1965

In the early morning I awoke with the last verse of Psalm 121: "The Lord will preserve thy going out and thy coming in from this time forth, and even for evermore". Also with Psalm 97, v. 8: "Zion heard, and was glad; and the daughters of Judah rejoiced because of thy judgements, O Lord". The sorrows of this judgement often coincide with the joys of the Church, as when Pharaoh and his hosts were drowned, but the daughters of Judah sang and danced before the Lord, who had delivered them from so great a peril. It may be that the remnant who fear the Lord in this age may, in a similar manner, have reason to praise His name in the midst of all the desolations which are to appear in the earth.

November 26, 1965

My dear friend, Mr Hugh MacQueen, Aberdeen, died suddenly last night. During the last few weeks he expressed the fear that he might still be an unsaved sinner. But I have reason to believe that behind his fears there was "a good hope through grace". (2 *Thessalonians* 2: 16) Also, before being told of his death, I awoke at night with these words in my mouth: "Gather my saints together unto me; those that have made a covenant with me by sacrifice". (*Ps.* 50: 5) Later today I mentioned my impression that one of the Lord's people had been taken Home. I was touched when his son then told me over the telephone that, with his last breath, my friend had expressed his faith his Redeemer.

Spoke recently of 'Christ's hospital' where all His people are, in this pained life. But in His hospital no one dies. Their sickness is not unto death.

December 10, 1965

Read *The Varieties of Religious Experience* by William James. Some experiences recorded in this book have their source in knowledge of God, while others obviously have their source in mere nature, if not in a subtle association with one who can transform himself into an angel of light. The whole book is scholarly but the field covered is difficult, and not altogether approached from the right angle. Instead of beginning with the varied experiences of the saints as these are portrayed in God's Word, he wanders over a wide area where the good, or what is consistent with Scripture, is mixed up with the bad. But the book has value in proving that the supernatural world is as real as, and more real than, the world of sense perception.

December 21, 1965

Reading a book called *More Than Notion*. Was deeply impressed by the words of a dying young woman, whose name was Matilda. "Where', she asked, 'is the passage, 'Praise waiteth for thee, O God, in Zion'? That is what I feel like just now: praise waits in my heart. I cannot express how this desire to praise is stretching its neck and ready to burst forth because of the Lord's mercy to me." (*Ps.* 65: 1) A friend then told her that the phrase in the *Epistle to the Romans*, "the earnest expectation

of the creature waiteth for the manifestation of the sons of God"
means exactly, "the stretching forth of the neck". (*Rom.* 8: 19)
The instinct to praise the Lord is present in the new creature.
There is also a longing in the gracious soul to get to that place
where praise is perfected.

1966

January 5, 1966

The New Year time has passed, with all its domestic bustle.
Last night as I was writing the words, "the good will of him
that dwelt in the bush", my heart was deeply touched and
melted down. I was in the act of writing a letter to a friend, and,
in quoting these words, I felt overwhelmed by the presence
of Him to Whom the words refer. (*Deut.* 33: 16) Immediately
I went outside and paced for a time in front of the church,
breathing out my longing for the day when I could love and
praise Him without the oppressive burden of sin. Afterwards
when I retired to rest I heard in my sleep these words being
sung beautifully:
"Whom have I in the heavens high
but thee, O Lord, alone?
And in the earth whom I desire,
besides thee there is none." (*Ps.* 73: 25)

My sleep, like the waking hours, was then sweet to me. Lord,
give me the grace to rest my affections on Thyself above all.

January 17, 1966

The recent death of a much loved friend, the Rev Duncan
Morrison, Free Church minister of Duirinish in Skye from 1932
to 1957, has filled me with sorrow. At his funeral, in the old
Gairloch cemetery, I was conscious of the Lord's presence. A
deep calm seemed to grace the service, and something like a
touch of summer prevailed during our walk to the grave. My
late father was his assistant in Skye for many years, and he
could not conceal his deep spiritual affection for Mr. Morrison.
Another soldier of Jesus Christ has "fallen asleep". (1 *Cor.* 15:
18) He is now beholding the face of Christ, and singing 'the new
song' of the redeemed within the portals of everlasting glory.

February 23, 1966

The Rev Hugh Mackay, minister of Aberdeen Free Church, preached here at the Communion services. Last night we had a discussion of the different ways in which God may converse spiritually with His people. He said his Aunt Charlotte seldom awoke in the morning but the word of the Lord was in her mouth. This is something of which I have some knowledge; but it is also something which has not entered the experience of all, or even many, of God's people. The Lord has other ways of refreshing the souls of His people. The longer I live, however, the more mysterious and awe-inspiring this spiritual experience becomes.

March 24, 1966

Had been over in the island of Scalpay at the Communion. In Stornoway felt the breath of the Spirit touching my soul in the Prayer meeting. Was able to leave "a word in season" with some. (*Is.* 50: 4)[44]

April 5, 1966

Deeply affected this morning, and yesterday, in reading the first chapter in Luke's *Gospel*. The different songs sung by men, women and angels, have their different notes of ecstasy, joy and wonder, in relation to the dawn of an eternal day, through the rising of the Sun of Righteousness. Felt as if I would like

---

44 'About this time... I was standing outside our manse door ...repeating to myself the words of Psalm 90... when a deep sense of God's presence, and the awe of His being, took possession of my soul. The words were... "For a thousand years in Thy sight are as but yesterday when it is past, and as a watch in the night." There I stood still with my head bowed. Time was like something that had ceased to be. I felt like one whose existence was in the eternal present, where the unchangeable ... God was the only Reality. All the events and all the inhabitants of time, from its beginning to its end, had, I felt, faded out like a mere dream... The irrelevance and transitoriness of all created things impressed my spirit beyond what I could describe.' (M 107-108)

to share in this great joy. How empty are the so-called 'joys' of this world compared to that joy which is "unspeakable and full of glory". (1 *Peter* 1: 8)

Prepared a sermon on the words of Psalm 89, v. 15, "Blessed are the people who know the joyful sound". The subject I found so pleasant that I wrote down my thoughts. I have not done any sermon-writing before.

June 8, 1966

The decisions of the Church of Scotland to continue their 'church unity' talks, and to admit women into the Eldership of the Church, are ominous. In all the speeches delivered in Assembly on both subjects, the Word of God as 'the final court of appeal' was not mentioned. The 'Church' is going to do everything in its own wise way 'and as the Holy Spirit will direct it'. As if the Spirit of God would initiate movements which are contrary to His own Word. This deep deception and presumption on the part of men who are wise in their own conceits has now become so entrenched in this Church that nothing, apart from the power of God, can take it away. We hope that voices may yet be heard within the Church of Scotland which shall strive to proclaim the truth of God's holy Word and arrest the present trends.

About twelve years ago God came near to me in the words of *Isaiah* 54, vs. 9-10, but not until now have I fully grasped the solemn implications of His great promise. "For this is as the waters of Noah unto me: for as I have sworn that the waters of Noah should no more go over the earth; so have I sworn that I would not be wroth with thee, nor rebuke thee. For the mountains shall depart, and the hills be removed, but my kindness shall not depart from thee, neither shall the covenant of my peace be removed, saith the Lord that hath mercy on thee." His oath stands, I hope, between me and my ill deservings. His everlasting love and faithfulness are wrapped up within it. O Lord, enable me to fix my eyes on this bright star of promise in all life's storms.

June 17, 1966

Last night I could not stay my mind upon God. I cried to Him to send me a word to comfort and compose my heart and mind. He heard my prayer, for in the morning I awoke repeating the words, "Oh how great is thy goodness, which thou hast laid up for them that fear thee". (*Ps.* 31: 19) I was enabled to look beyond "things seen" to the Treasure which God has laid up for His own people in Heaven. (2 *Cor.* 4: 18) This Treasure is Himself.

The words, "Woe to them that are at ease in Zion", speak loudly to the Lord's people in this day of rebuke and blasphemy. (*Amos* 6: 1) I can truly say before God that the need that His cause might be revived is a heavy burden on my spirit. And I made the discovery that when, in my poor prayers, I plead for the welfare of Zion, my heart melts and I feel that the Lord enables me to cry to Him, that He might raise her again out of the dust.

July 19, 1966

My dear friend, Rev Roderick Murray, minister at Skerray in Caithness, assisted us at the communion last weekend. Was deeply impressed by his nearness to the Lord and by his devotion to His service. His sermons made an impression on the people. One felt that his whole heart was present in every word.

Met a young woman to whom I spoke several years ago with regard to her soul. God blessed the word to her. There are few joys in my life compared to that of meeting my spiritual children, those whom the Lord called by His Spirit into His kingdom.

August 16, 1966

Home from the island of Skye. For several days I mourned over the silence of the Lord to my soul. But He refreshed my soul through the powerful and sweet application of the 23rd and 24th verses of Psalm 22. "Ye that fear the Lord, praise him; all ye the seed of Jacob, glorify him; and fear him, all ye the seed of Israel. For he hath not despised nor abhorred the affliction of the afflicted; neither hath he hid his face from him; but when he cried unto him, he heard."

During one of my walks on the road to Glendale, in Skye, the Lord gave me an overwhelming sense of His presence, as I sang and meditated on the beginning of Psalm 90: "Lord, thou hast been our dwelling place in all generations".

Read a beautifully written article in the current Free Church *Monthly Record* on 'Ealasaid Ruadh' of Stratherrick, Inverness-shire. This very godly woman had certain experiences which I could understand and follow. The brief portrayal of her life was a well of comfort to me. Felt my heart bound to this dear woman in whose suffering spirit God dwelt.

Since coming home, my sleep has been sweet to me. For the last three nights God's Word was present with me in the night watches. It was the subject of my song, conversation and prayers. How melodiously did I sing the 19th verse of Psalm 118 in my sleep! "Open to me the gates of righteousness: I will go into them, and I will praise the Lord". It was as if my younger voice had returned.

September 8, 1966

Spent the weekend at Aberdeen where I 'introduced' our son-in-law, Mr J. Douglas MacMillan, on Sabbath morning. In the evening he preached an excellent sermon on *Romans* 1, v. 16: "For I am not ashamed of the gospel of Christ: for it is the power of God unto salvation to every one that believeth; to the Jew first, and also to the Greek". May the Lord set the seal of His approval on his ministry. Our dear Mary and her family should be happy in Aberdeen.

Had several encouraging letters from some far and near about my book *In All Their Affliction*. The Lord knows that there is in my heart a true desire to comfort His people with the comfort wherewith I myself am comforted of God.

September 23, 1966

Two friends died in Inverness. Before I heard about it, the Lord spoke to me in the words, "As for man, his days are as grass; as a flower of the field so he flourisheth".

This morning also I was arrested by the words, "For in the time of trouble he shall hide me in his pavilion". (*Ps.* 27: 5) Lord, cover Thou my head in a day of trouble.

October 14, 1966

Had a brief talk with our local schoolmaster last night on the brevity of life and the danger of letting irrelevant, intellectual interests take the place of God. His preoccupation with philosophy eats up so much of his time. God, in His Word and our salvation, should be the 'Alpha and Omega' of our life. While we all have our subordinate interests, our preparation for the eternal world should have priority, and we should realise its urgency. "Set thine house in order, for thou shalt surely die." (2 *Kings* 20: 1)

October 26, 1966

Visited Aberdeen. Had the pleasure of listening to our son-in-law Douglas MacMillan twice on Sabbath. I would describe his sermons as lucid, powerful and edifying. I would say that the atmosphere in the church on Sabbath morning was solemn and warm. Took a Gaelic service in the afternoon.

November 11, 1966

Greatly distressed over one of our ministers who has left our Church because he insisted that some of his remarks over Sabbath desecration were misunderstood or misinterpreted. But he proved to be most unreasonable. He would not submit to the admonitions of his brethren, even when our approach to him was brotherly and affectionate. I thank God that after thirty-six years in the ministry I was, by the grace of God, enabled to refrain from a spirit of contention or discord. May the Lord enable me so to continue to the end.

Had a letter from the Rev D. Mackenzie of Castletown, asking me to consider a call to Caithness. I was surprised that they should think of a man of my age. Brought the matter before the Lord in prayer: "Thy will be done". (*Mat.* 6: 10)

Awoke a few mornings ago with the words,
"The Lord hath me chastised sore,
but not to death given over." (*Ps.* 118: 18)

O Lord, if Thy rod of chastisement is again to be on my soul or body, give me the grace to endure it. Let Thy love be mixed in with "the waters of Marah", to sweeten them for my soul. (*Ex.* 15: 23)

My seasons of private prayer have been most sweet for the last while. No sooner do I bow my head in the Lord's presence than I become quite melted down in my soul. How easy it is to pray when His dew rests upon one's spirit. I could say that He could not deny my love to Him, and – so my feelings went – that I could not love Him more than I did; although I know I ought to love Him infinitely more. Ah, how little can the poor earthen vessel hold of this fullness. Nothing can purify the heart like the love of Christ, and nothing else can show us the comparative worthlessness of all created things. God is all I want. With Him I am satisfied. Lord, embrace this sinner, and make me fit to proclaim Thy praise forever in Thine own presence.

December 1, 1966

Last night, while I was writing a letter, I used the words, "God is love. Short of this there is nothing, and beyond this there is nothing". (1 *John* 4: 8) What I meant was that without God and His love, our future here and throughout eternity holds nothing but desolation, emptiness and grief. When I wrote these words I was transported in my own soul. But Satan was near. He threw one of his fiery darts into my mind, in the form of an evil thought. Instantly my sun went down, and my "prosperous state was turned into misery". The Lord warned me by His Word soon afterwards, "lest I should be exalted above measure". (2 *Cor.* 12: 7) But He did not leave me there, for He also said, "My grace is sufficient for thee". (2 *Cor.* 12: 9) The Lord was afterwards pleased to comfort me through the words,

"For this God doth abide
Our God for evermore; he will
even unto death us guide." (*Ps.* 48: 14)

1967

January 4, 1967

The passing away of Mr Mackay, Watten, in Caithness, and Mr Campbell, Nairn, has deeply affected me.[45] The latter was the friend of my younger days in Greenock. He was a guileless and affectionate man. Was led to preach on the words, "With gladness and rejoicing they shall be brought: they shall enter into the King's palace". (*Ps.* 45: 15) Of all the sermons I preached in Resolis, this one touched my own heart most. I could not help mentioning Mr Campbell's name during my remarks.

February 18, 1967

The severe spiritual trials through which I have passed for several weeks now have left me somewhat weakened in body and disturbed in spirit. The Lord, however, was gracious in upholding me by His Word and, I hope, by His gracious presence. He visited me with two precious promises from the Psalms. One was from Psalm 18, v. 46: "The Lord liveth; and blessed be my rock; and let the God of my salvation be exalted". The other was from Psalm 91, v. 4: "his truth shall be thy shield and buckler". How appropriate were these words to my distressed soul. "Who is a God like unto thee, that pardoneth iniquity, and passeth by the transgression of the remnant of his heritage? He retaineth not his anger for ever, because he delighteth in mercy." (*Micah* 7: 18)

March 23, 1967

Two nights in succession I awoke with God's Word very sweetly on my lips. The first night I dreamt that I was present in a company and that, in a voice full of melody and power, I began to sing the words:

45 This may have been a Mr Peter Campbell from Skye, who was a friend in Greenock.

"Then are they glad, because at rest
and quiet now they be:
So to the haven he them brings,
which they desired to see." (*Ps.* 107: 30)

This morning, again, I dreamt that I was in Heaven, and that
I began to sing the words:

"They shall be brought with gladness great,
and mirth on every side,
Into the palace of the King
and there they shall abide." (*Ps.* 45: 15)

I saw our daughter Mary among the people who were there.
These are pleasant, if mysterious, visitations.

March 31, 1967

I had been at the Communion with my cousin the Rev
Malcolm Morrison, minister of Partick Highland Free Church,
where I myself laboured for seventeen years. Rev Wallace Bruce
Nicholson was there also.[46] I felt that the Lord was present at
some of the services. I especially enjoyed the Sabbath evening
service in Gaelic. The large Church was full. My theme was, "If
thou knewest the gift of God, and who it is that saith to thee,
Give me to drink; thou wouldest have asked of him, and he
would have given thee living water". (*John* 4: 10) It was good
to meet so many of the old friends again. But some have passed
away.

Visited the Rev William Campbell, formerly of Lewis, who is
dying. Felt as if the Lord was present in the room as we prayed
together. His many and deep sorrows, we believe, are now at
an end.

46 Mr Nicholson was Minister of Scalpay Free Church from 1955 to 1961,
and of Plockton and Kyle Free Church from 1961 to 1970.

May 1, 1967

A few evenings ago at Fortrose, in the Black Isle, I listened to an impressive sermon on the words, "But the greatest of these is love". (I *Cor.* 13, v. 13) A true mark of love to God is an approval and an adoration of all that He is and does. Whether we think of Him in His Being, in His grace or in His judgements, He is altogether desirable and "lovely". The true believer justifies Him in all His providential dealings with him. Whatever trials may emerge in our lot or life here we say, "Good is the will; and good is the hand of the Lord". "Though He slay me, yet will I trust Him." (*Job* 13: 15) Yes, and love Him too. A graceless person may have something like 'cupboard love' to God; but this is a false 'love' which perishes with its first contact with adversity or with the removal of earthly comforts or riches. This 'love' is really hatred in disguise. Only the righteous love Him.

May 9, 1967

This morning as I went to the Church hall where I often "call on the name of the Lord" I felt an aversion to my spiritual duties rising up within me. (*Ps.* 116: 17) There were also many inferior demands on my time. But I struggled hard against this barrier; and when at last I bowed my head before the Lord I felt a wave of His love and goodwill passing over my spirit. It was sweet and easy to pray then. The Lord enabled me to pray for His diminished Cause, that He might again come down "like rain on the mown grass" (*Ps.* 72: 6) and give His people "a little reviving in their bondage". (*Ezra* 9: 8)

June 7, 1967

For two days I laboured under much fear over the present Middle East crisis. Prayed earnestly that the Lord would preserve His Israel, to whom He is still bound in His covenant and promise, and who are still "beloved for the fathers' sakes". (*Rom.* 11: 28) During our Prayer meeting last night a strange and strong conviction took possession of my mind and heart that their enemies, though more numerous than they, were being subdued. My heart rejoiced. And throughout this day I was deeply aware of the Lord's presence. I found the words, "And they returned to Jerusalem with great joy", sweet beyond words. (*Luke* 24: 52) This new deliverance of God's ancient people is another proof that their Heavenly Guardian is still on their side. Lord, give me to pray that the day may soon come when they shall be quickened by Thy Spirit, and come to know their Messiah, the Lord Jesus Christ.

July 18, 1967

Another of our ministers has brought a shadow over our Church through his indiscretion. Lord, keep me from doing Thy Cause in this world any harm, or from grieving Thy people and Thy Spirit through any gross outward misbehaviour. This has been my prayer and concern ever since I came to profess the Lord's name.

Yesterday morning I was again deeply touched by the first verses of Psalm 57: "yea, in the shadow of thy wings will I make my refuge, until these calamities be overpast...He shall send from heaven, and save me from the reproach of him that would swallow me up". The words remained with me all day and, in a way I cannot describe, I felt that I was under the wings of The Eternal. It was strange that I should read this morning about a similar experience told of Thomas Jolly, a Puritan father. "One night about this time", he records, "I had such a dream as I could not but take notice of; I was led along through a dark valley into a most sumptuous temple where I was inconceivably ravished in spirit, and was raised to sing part of the 25th Psalm, verses 5-6, to a tune inexpressibly melodious... so that I seemed to have a taste of the celestial state above."

"...And do thou lead me in thy truth,
therein my teacher be:
For thou art God that dost
to me salvation send,

And I upon thee all the day
expecting do attend.
Thy tender mercies, Lord,
I pray thee to remember,
And loving-kindnesses; for they
have been of old for ever."

July 30, 1967

Was much exercised during the night with the words, "O taste and see that the Lord is good". (*Ps.* 34: 8) I seemed to be addressing a company of people and telling them that David, with all his gifts and with all his powers which enabled him to describe the joys and the sorrows of the people of God, found one theme beyond all speech. It was the unspeakable blessedness of God communicating Himself to the soul. Only in Heaven, I believe, will we be able to express this sense of "joy unspeakable" which the presence of God brings into the heart of man. (1 *Peter* 1: 8)

A few nights ago I dreamt again that I was in a company whose garments excelled in loveliness all beauty I have seen on earth. I awoke singing again, not with my lips but in my heart, the words:

"Instead of those thy fathers dear,
thy children thou mayest take,
And in all places of the earth
them noble princes make." (*Ps.* 45: 16)

Lord, Thou knowest that this has been the subject of my prayers over the years. I thought it also a remarkable coincidence that at that very hour, about 7.00 a.m., our daughter Mary's little boy entered this world.

October 10, 1967

Very concerned over the Lord's silence to my soul. "How long wilt thou forget me, O Lord?" (*Ps.* 13: 1) May I be led to discern why the Beloved withdraws Himself. My sin is ever before me; but I do not want to grieve the Spirit or alienate the Lord's presence from my soul.

The doctor wants me to see a specialist in Inverness to find out the cause of my present physical infirmity. It has been with me now for many months. I shall be entering hospital soon, and may have to undergo an operation. I leave myself, soul and body, in the hand of the Lord.

November 27, 1967

Returned home from Inverness last Tuesday. I underwent an operation which, I am told, was quite 'successful'.

A few hours before the operation I was very conscious of the Lord's presence. I also felt that many of His dear people were praying for me. These words touched my soul in a wonderful way that I cannot describe: "Come, ye blessed of my Father, inherit the kingdom prepared for you from the foundation of the world". (*Mat.* 25: 34) I felt that, whatever might happen to my poor mortal frame, my life was hid with Christ in God, and that He would bring me, great sinner though I am, to that blessed place where "the inhabitant shall not say, I am sick". (*Is.* 33: 24)

December 29, 1967

My present indisposition has left me spiritually listless. My discomfort is at the same time both a distraction and an oppression. But it should not be. If I were more spiritually-minded, and my faith more in exercise, I should, like Paul, glory in infirmities. I am far removed from those who, over long seasons on beds of pain, remain in the path of duty, who also pray without ceasing, and retain their nearness to The Lord. I try to emerge out of this dull listless state only to sink again into a cold silent region. There are moments, however, when I do feel The Lord's Word touching my heart, like rays of light through the clouds.

1968

March 19, 1968

Our recent Communion was to my soul a time of refreshing. The Rev Malcolm MacLean, Lochcarron, Wester Ross assisted us over the weekend. The atmosphere in the Church was unusually solemn and warm. Still confined to the house, more or less, and my physical discomfort continues. Had a visit this morning from my dear friend in the Lord, Mr W. Macdonald, Munlochy, in the Black Isle. How pleasant to meet one of the Lord's people in a day when His witnesses are so few.

March 25, 1968

This morning I awoke in a state of much consolation. Had been dreaming that I was in the company of a man who sang in a lovely voice the first verse of Psalm 85:
"Jacob's captivity thou hast
recalled with mighty hand."

In the evening I had preached, with a measure of freedom, my first sermon in five months. I was surprised that my mind and body were none the worse for the exertion; for I went to the service in fear and trembling.

Rev Hugh Ferrier of Crow Road Free Church, Glasgow, insisted on seeing some of my sermons when he called here a few months ago. Now our Publications Committee are interested in them. May the Lord be glorified, and His dear people edified and comforted through my poor efforts.[47]

Nothing affects my heart now more than my confession of God at the Throne of Grace. My heart is awed and solemnized in whatever way I think of Him, whether it be in His glorious attributes, His revelation of Himself in The Word, or His nearness, love, and compassion for His people in every age.

47 Murdo Campbell published two volumes of original sermons, entitled *Everlasting Love* (Edinburgh 1968: The Knox Press) and *No Night There* (Stornoway 1973: Stornoway Religious Bookshop).

An indescribable desire and longing to enjoy and praise Him for ever sometimes overwhelms me. Satan would make me believe that all this is mere emotion which is the result of my present bodily infirmity; but nothing else affects me in this way. Only my sweet thoughts of God.

May 2, 1968

This morning I awoke with these words, "For our heart shall rejoice in him, because we have trusted in his holy name ". (*Ps.* 33: 21) These words from the lips of the Beloved both refreshed my soul and reassured me that, notwithstanding all my fears, lapses and provocations, He is still near and mindful of me in my afflictions.

May 13, 1968

Preached yesterday with a measure of strength and freedom such as I have not enjoyed for some months now. On Thursday I attended a local funeral. About two hundred men were present, many of whom I never see in God's house. At our prayer meetings two or three men are present. The rest are women. What an ominous sign this is! The dead burying their dead, while the means of grace are largely neglected.

This morning I awoke in a state of great comfort with the words on my lips, "he will rest in his love". (*Zephanaiah* 3: 17) The more I thought of these words the more amazed I was at the wonderful condescension of God, who makes His own Zion, and the hearts of His people, His place of rest. If I could love Him more, and serve Him better!

May 26, 1968

How rapidly we move toward God's judgments! I cannot help associating my fear at what is coming with the words with which God awoke me out of sleep this morning:

"Only thou with thine eyes shall look,
  and a beholder be;

And thou therein the just reward
of wicked men shall see." (*Ps.* 91: 8)

June 17, 1968

Sitting recently in the Loch Maree Hotel I saw a young couple
whose faces expressed something which, I felt, was not of this
world. When I spoke to them I discovered that they loved and
feared the Lord. Though our meeting was only momentary I
knew that we would meet in a better world where we would
part no more. It is the love of Christ "shed abroad in our hearts"
that unites God's people to one another. (*Rom.* 5: 5)

Reading the *Life of Madame Guyon*, whose nearness
to God and resignation to His Will, amid all her trials and
afflictions, made me bow my head. God's love, His word and
presence sustained her to the end. Like a lily among thorns she
maintained her witness for Christ and His Word. The forces of
darkness failed to put out her candle amid all her persecutions.

August 27, 1968

Back from Stornoway. Spoke to a girl about Christ's
conversation with the woman of Samaria about "the gift of
God", which is "the water of life". (*John* 4: 10) Afterwards the
Matron of the Home where she worked told me that earlier the
words, "And he must needs go through Samaria" impressed
themselves on her mind, and that one of the girls who worked
in the Home, and for whom she had often prayed, then told her
about 'the minister' who exhorted her to read Christ's words to
the woman at the well of Sychar. (*John* 4: 4) She believed the
word of exhortation was blessed to the girl's soul.

Had been mourning over my spiritual deadness for some
days. The Lord was silent apart from a word that brought more
concern than comfort. Yesterday, however, He drew very near
to me in the words of Psalm 16, verses 2 and 3: "...my goodness
extended not to thee; but to the saints that are in the earth, and
to the excellent, in whom is all my delight". All day I felt my

soul going out in unspeakable love to the Lord and to all His people in Heaven and on earth.

September 21, 1968

This afternoon I felt that I should go aside to offer a brief prayer. No sooner did I bow my head in the secret place than I felt God's love and presence touching me at the depth of my heart and making me say, "Yea, Lord; thou knowest that I love thee". (*John* 21: 15) The sweetness, comfort and blessedness of this enjoyment are still with me. O, that it might remain with me to the end.

Was in Dingwall a few evenings ago where I listened to an impressive and powerful sermon from my son-in-law Douglas MacMillan, from Aberdeen. May the Lord spare him to proclaim His precious Gospel in this sad age of spiritual decline. Dear Mary, his wife, is with us here for a few days.

Visited Inverness where we hope to spend the evening of our days. A house in Grigor Drive appealed to us both and there, God willing, we may settle down. I have not yet recovered from my recent illness, and I feel that I should now go aside and rest a while. My prayer is, "Abide with us, for it is toward evening and the day is far spent". (*Luke* 24: 29)

November 30, 1968

We are now resident in Inverness. The strain of 'flitting' is more or less over. We were sorry to leave Resolis where we spent seventeen quiet and happy years, and where we lived among a kind and peaceable people. The Lord comforted me by His Word just before we left: "O, God, when thou wentest forth before thy people, when thou didst march through the wilderness". (*Ps.* 68: 7) We worship in Greyfriars Free Church where the Rev Donald MacDonald is exercising a useful ministry. My book of sermons, *Everlasting Love*, is well received and commended in all evangelical circles. May the Lord bless this poor effort to His own glory. For the last while I have been writing notes on a verse or two in each Psalm, words from the Songs of Zion which had been blessed to myself. My health is still somewhat indifferent. Had a kind letter today from Rev H. Carson, editor of the *Gospel Magazine*, asking me to provide him with a few sermons for publication. Greatly affected by the words, "Acquaint now thyself with him". (*Job* 22: 21)[48]

---

48 Murdo Campbell wrote seventeen books and pamphlets. Many were reprinted; some were translated, most of them into Dutch.

1969

January 28, 1969

Was back in hospital for ten days for some treatment and what is called a 'check-up'. Felt somewhat disturbed over the conduct and conversation of some of the patients. Others, however, were kind and well-mannered. The nurses and doctors in attendance were most kind and considerate.

Had a letter from Rev Iain Murray, of the *Banner of Truth* Press, asking me to send him some material suitable for publication. He is interested in my notes on the Psalms.

Rev Duncan Leitch, minister of Dingwall Free Church, told of a nurse who said a letter and book she had from a minister in Ross-shire, 'a Mr Campbell', were the means of bringing her back from her association with the Mormons. I was happy to hear of this. This young woman's aunt had asked me to warn and exhort her with regard to her spiritual danger. And God blessed our prayers.

Attended meetings in the Free North Church. I was deeply impressed by two sermons preached by an able young man, the Rev Donald MacLeod of Kilmallie, Inverness-shire.[49]

February 9, 1969

Motored over to Resolis on Friday last for my 'retirement presentation'. It was a sad occasion, though I could not but appreciate the great kindness of the people.

Amid all my fears and infirmities the Lord has comforted me by applying His sweet and precious Word to my soul, on two nights in succession. First, "Love never faileth" (1 *Cor.* 13: 8) Then, "Remember the word unto thy servant, upon which thou hast caused me to hope". (*Ps.* 119: 49) I have no comfort in this world but God's blessed Word. I hope I have received it

49 The Revd Prof. Donald MacLeod, D.D., subsequently minister of Partick Highland Free Church in Glasgow (where Murdo Campbell had ministered for seventeen years); Principal of the Free Church College, where he was also Professor of Systematic Theology.

as my "heritage for ever". Reminded also in the night watches that our dear Lord Himself was upheld in all His sorrows by the Eternal Father. "Behold my servant whom I uphold." (*Is.* 42: 1) The same love is exercised in relation to His suffering people.

March 27, 1969

Felt much refreshed and encouraged by awaking two mornings ago with the words, "the Lord hath dealt bountifully with thee." (*Ps.* 116: 7) An equally precious experience was in reading a comment by 'Archie' Cook on the words, "he will rest in his love". (*Zephaniah* 3: 17)[50] He spoke of God resting in the finished work of His Son, and of all those for whom Christ died finding rest only in what Christ did in His finished work. This is where, in the words of Zephaniah, God sings over His people with joy.

May 22, 1969

Through my prolonged physical discomfort my nerves are, at the moment, somewhat frayed. For several weeks I felt somewhat depressed, and I was afraid that I had grieved the Spirit of the Lord by my sins. My "sins and faults of youth" (*Ps.* 25: 7) brought me into the depths of fear and anxiety; and I could not get away from the words, "Against thee, thee only, have I sinned". (*Ps.* 51: 4) But the Lord saw my tears and, I hope, heard my prayer. Two mornings ago I awoke very conscious of His presence and with these words on my lips, "The eternal God is thy refuge, and underneath are the everlasting arms". (*Deut.* 33: 27) My comfort was so deep that I could not speak. The wonder and the awe of God's nearness and grace I cannot describe. "Who is a God like unto thee, that pardoneth iniquity..." (*Micah* 7: 18)

---

50 The Revd Archibald Cook was Minister of the North Church, Inverness from 1837 to 1844, and of Daviot Free Church, Inverness-shire, from 1844 to 1865.

May 30, 1969

This morning just before waking I was greatly impressed listening, in a lovely dream, to a man who sang the first and the last verses of Psalm 23. "The Lord is my shepherd; I shall not want...Surely goodness and mercy shall follow me all the days of my life: and I will dwell in the house of the Lord for ever." It was sung in a voice such as one cannot hear in this world. The Lord is kind to me these days in comforting me through His blessed Word. He is truly the Comforter of the afflicted soul, and the Brother born for adversity.

May 31, 1969

This morning again, at about the same time, I was much comforted by the words, "And he led them forth by the right way, that they might go to a city of habitation". (*Ps.* 107: 7)

June 10, 1969

Last Sabbath morning I was greatly refreshed by an unforgettable sense of God's sweet Presence. I seemed to be in a new world, a world of beauty and peace. Verse 17 of Psalm 45 was present with me in a way that brought me much assurance and consolation. "I will make thy name to be remembered in all generations: therefore shall the people praise thee for ever and ever". Afterwards I recalled that these were the words with which my beloved father left this world of time: "I will make thy name to be remembered in all generations".

August 29, 1969

The last verse of Psalm 40 was a great comfort to me for the past two days. "But I am poor and needy; yet the Lord thinketh upon me: thou art my help and my deliverer; make no tarrying, O my God." As usual, it touched my soul during the night. After one of our recent Prayer meetings I was refreshed by my contacts with several dear Christian friends. Over the years of my Christian pilgrimage I have often made the discovery that God's people are the only people on earth in whose company I am happy.

Greatly refreshed again by the words, "And he led them forth by the right way that they might go to a city of habitation". (*Ps.* 107: 7) My heart also leaped with joy when I remembered that God sealed these words on my heart a few months ago, as my Diary reminds me. His Word is my only comfort.

But how distressing our life can be in retrospect! I discover that what gave me no concern in other days is now a source of grief to me. If the Lord loves us He will chasten us for all we think, say and do contrary to His holy will. A few nights ago I dreamt that I was in the company of an elderly man who looked very downcast. As I stood before him I quoted the words, "Whom the Lord loveth he chasteneth, and scourgeth every son whom he receiveth". (*Heb.* 12: 6) Then, instead of becoming more sad-looking, his holy face radiated joy. I felt on awaking that by this night visit the Lord would have me to rejoice in His chastening hand since, if I am His, this is one evidence of His interest in me. But what grace we need to submit uncomplainingly to His rod; especially if we are disposed by temperament to feelings of depression, for example, at times.

October 26, 1969

Deeply touched by the words, "...for there shall be no night there". (*Rev.* 21: 25) Took upon myself to make a few comments on these words at our recent Prayer meeting. I could see that others were affected by them also. Heaven is a nightless world. There is no night of sin, ignorance, sorrow, temptation, fear, loneliness or death there.

Yesterday Mrs Tallach, who owns the Religious Bookshop in Dingwall, told me that she was going to produce a new edition of my book, *Gleanings of Highland Harvest* (Glasgow 1953: N. Adshead & Son Ltd; also Tain, Ross-shire and Houston, Texas, 1957: Christian Focus Publications.). This book has had a large circulation, and has been much appreciated by Christian people in various places.

Enjoyed my secret prayer and meditation for the last few days, but now I fear my sins cause the Lord to remove His presence from my soul.

November 11, 1969

Three ministers of our Church, whom I knew well, have recently passed away. One was my friend during my brief ministry in Fort Augustus, the Rev Malcolm Galbraith. He was a good and kindly man.[51] Another was Rev Donald Fraser, who was my College contemporary. Humble and self-conscious, he remained almost all his ministerial life in the tiny congregation of Aberfeldy, Perthshire.[52] Another much younger friend, the Rev John MacDonald, of Gravir, Lewis, in the fullness of strength, fell dead outside his manse yesterday. Both he and his wife were in my congregation in Glasgow. John was a holy man whose life testified that God was his companion during his pilgrimage here. It was remarkable that the previous day he had preached from the words, "Henceforth there is laid up for me a crown of righteousness..." (2 *Timothy* 4: 8)

Enjoyed a much-needed refreshing from the words of Psalm 84, vs. 8-9. "O Lord God of hosts, hear my prayer: give ear, O God of Jacob. *Selah.* Behold, O God our shield, and look upon the face of thine anointed". God's presence touched my soul with these words; also with words in Psalm 118, v. 15 (first part): "The voice of rejoicing and salvation is in the tabernacles of the righteous".

51 Mr Galbraith was latterly Minister of Kirkcaldy Free Church from 1950 to 1963. As Minister of Fort William and Kilmonivaig he was a fellow-presbyter of Murdo Campbell's during his ministry in Fort Augustus and Glenmoriston.

52 The Revd Donald Fraser's brother, the Revd Alexander Fraser, was Free Church Minister in Kilwinning, Ayrshire when he married Peggy, Murdo Campbell's younger sister.

November 28, 1969

In reading the Book of *Job* I was deeply affected by the words, "But none saith, where is God my maker, who giveth songs in the night". (*Job* 35: 10) There have been many nights in my life when God solemnized, refreshed and upheld my spirit in such a way. To me it is a deep and real spiritual experience, if full of mystery, that the Holy Spirit, Who dwells in His people, can instruct and converse with them, not only when they are awake, but when, like Jacob, they are asleep on their pillow.

1970

January 24, 1970

This morning I was refreshed by another drop from Heaven: "He turned the rock into standing water, the flint into a fountain of waters". (*Ps.* 114: 8) The words mean that God can change our afflictions into a means of comfort and blessings.

April 7, 1970

After a restless night I slept towards morning, and as often happens I awoke singing, inwardly, verse 24 of Psalm 73: "Thou, with thy counsel, while I live, wilt me conduct and guide; and to thy glory afterward receive me to abide". I was also dreaming that I was present in a company, one of whom was deeply affected by God's Word. Nothing brings me more joy than God's Word.

April 24, 1970

Last Monday evening I felt compelled to spend an hour in private devotion. No sooner did I find myself alone than these words touched my spirit with great power, consolation and awe, "But unto them that look for him shall he appear the second time without sin unto salvation". (*Heb.* 9: 28) I was like one who was instantly transported into another and infinitely better world.[53] I could say with another, "The Lord is in this

53 Murdo Campbell's notion of mystic 'transport' or 'rapture' contrasts in some ways with William James's. For James, rapture is ineffable and fleeting. (James 380) For an Evangelical Protestant also, such as Campbell, rapture is beyond words, yet tied to Scripture texts. It is also durable: he mentions "weeks" whose "afterglow" alone lasted "many days". (M 50) James adds that meditation is a method: one of St Ignatius's Spiritual Exercises replaces sensation with imagined holy scenes, and these in turn with rapture. (James 406-407) This method is ascetic, unlike Campbell's. Also, conjuring up images is not what 'meditating' usually means, and need not be theistic. Once rapture is attained, Campbell does not jettison the 'long hard training' of meditation. And to meditate on God's Word is to encounter Him unmediated by images, clergy or ritual.

place". (*Gen.* 28: 16) These words led me to many others which speak of that good hope of seeing the Lord as He is and where He is. They were especially associated with the words of the Bride in the *Song of Solomon*, 2, v. 17, "Until the day break, and the shadows flee away, turn, my beloved, and be thou like a roe or a young hart upon the mountains of Bether". How wonderful shall the eternal world be, where one day with the Lord shall be as a thousand years, and a thousand years as one day. Sweet beyond words was this hour, when I seemed like one who dwelt on the fringe of a world of unspeakable bliss. I had a feeling afterwards that some trial was on the way. And so it was. A family arrived at our door the following evening whose words greatly disturbed me. But the Lord, I know, shall uphold me to the end of my earthly pilgrimage.

May 27, 1970

It has pleased the Lord to seal His Word again on my poor distressed soul in the night watches and, as often happens, through the Psalms: "Oh how great is thy goodness, which thou hast laid up for them that fear thee". (*Ps.* 31: 19) "What shall I render unto the Lord for all his benefits toward me?" (*Ps.* 116: 12) And from Psalm 18, v. 46, "The Lord liveth; and blessed be my rock; and let the God of my salvation be exalted". If only I could retain and enjoy the comfort which is present in these precious words!

July 14, 1970

Last Sabbath morning, after a season of spiritual anxiety, the Lord spoke to me very vividly and comfortingly in the last verses of Psalm 43.[54] What could I do without His Word? Nothing but, in the words of David, perish in my many afflictions.

My book printed by the Banner of Truth Trust came into my hands today. The Lord bless its message, whatever its faults. The title is *From Grace to Glory* (London 1970)

December 2, 1970

Felt again somewhat discouraged over my latest literary effort; but during the hours of a recent night these words of Psalm 43: 5, in the metrical version, were present in my mind:
"Why art thou then cast down, my soul?
what should discourage thee?
And why with vexing thoughts art thou
disquieted in me?
Still trust in God; for Him to praise
good cause I yet shall have."

Then I got word that my book on the Psalms, *From Grace to Glory*, was a help and comfort to some who read it. In this I saw that in relation to my poor effort, the promises of God are "Yea and Amen" in His well-beloved Son.

Now having reached the day of promise, 'three score years and ten', I am happy that the Lord is still conversing with my soul.

O Lord, give me to finish my course here believing and knowing that "Thou art with me" (*Ps.* 23: 4) and that Thou art my portion for ever and ever. (*Ps.*73: 26)

54 "O send out thy light and thy truth: let them lead me; let them bring me unto thy holy hill, and to thy tabernacles. Then will I go unto the altar of God, unto God my exceeding joy; yea, upon the harp will I praise thee, O God my God. Why art thou cast down, O my soul? and why art thou disquieted within me? hope in God: for I shall yet praise him, who is the health of my countenance, and my God".

1971

December 22, 1971

This evening as I was looking at some of God's promises which He had so lovingly applied to my soul, I was deeply awed and affected on seeing I had noted in my Bible several months ago that He awoke me out of sleep with these unspeakably precious words, "Eye hath not seen, ear hath not heard, neither have entered into the heart of man, the things which God hath prepared for them that love him." (1 *Cor.* 2: 9) O, my God, may I, throughout eternity, go on making new and ever glorious discoveries of "the unsearchable riches of Christ". (*Eph.* 3: 8)

Newmills

Biographical Notes

1. Early life

Born in 1900 in Swainbost, in the district of Ness on the Isle of Lewis, Murdoch (or 'Murdo') Campbell grew up in a 'black' house, with a fire in the centre of the floor. His father, Alexander Campbell (1863-1947), was a crofter-fisherman and lay missionary. His mother, Christiana (1870-1933), had been a MacLean whose family was 'cleared' from Uig, Lewis, but settled in Swainbost with a different landlord. Two of Murdo's brothers, known locally as the 'Puilean' and 'Boxer', were acclaimed writers; so also are two of the Boxer's sons, Alistair and Norman.

Murdo's father once walked "many miles across the moor looking for a stray sheep. It was winter. As he sat down to rest for a moment he suddenly found himself on the fringe of another world. He lost all consciousness both of time and of his immediate surroundings. ...The glorious spiritual world which he had just entered he saw by faith." (*Memories of a Wayfaring Man* [M] p. 4)

On another occasion his father "engaged a boat to collect peats in a distant isle. Returning home, the heavily-loaded boat had to battle against a... rising storm... At last we were tossed behind a small island where we sheltered." They were reported lost, but one Calum MacLeod "sought counsel in prayer... [and] informed my anxious mother that before a certain hour that night she would welcome us at the door. A few minutes before the hour he mentioned we arrived at our home." (M 38)

As a child Murdo would "watch the huge concourse of people who passed by to Church services...The [Sabbath] day and the occasion were held in deep reverence". (M 8) And "family worship was observed in our home." (M 9)

A Lewis childhood could be idyllic. "During the summer school vacation we lived a carefree pastoral life. In the morning I would lead forth a number of the village cattle toward a lovely fringe of green pasture land which lay by the shore. There I would spend the day with only the sun to tell me the time, and the brook, the sea and the sand to provide me with pastime." (M 18)

2. Clairvoyance

As a boy however his knee became infected; at one point he was given up for dead. (M 19) Medication and pain relief were unavailable and, lying by the fire, unable to look outdoors, he routinely 'saw' what his siblings were reading in school half a mile away, and what games they played on the way home. They confirmed his claims but tried to discourage such an affront to ordinary, familiar assumptions. Thus his clairvoyance was not religious in origin; and it stayed with him until his health declined in old age.

Clairvoyance is not mysticism, but like mystical experience it seems to be given rather than achieved. The Diary supplies many examples. Almost daily some text or other might waken him early with spiritual assurance, or impress on him somehow that for example a friend, even overseas, had died. Later it would be confirmed that his experience had occurred at the moment of death. The timing was inexplicable, the accuracy many times greater than chance. Indeed without rhetoric, a story, or deceit, clairvoyance can support Scripture texts. Yet it need not support theism, and he ignored such experiences unless backed by a text. They did not concern only the personal, or bad news, or the moment. When few believed that Britain could win the Second World War, he dreamt that God would destroy Hitler, and wrote to a grateful Churchill.

Incidents like these both reveal and call into question ordinary beliefs concerning the relation between mind and body. The infection cost him years of schooling and a coveted place in the Navy; he joined the Army instead, though the war ended a month later, and he saw no combat. He went on to become a shipwright in Greenock.

He recalls the Iolaire disaster. "On a grey and stormy New Year's morning in 1919 we were shocked to hear that many sailors, including two of my companions, all happy to be home, perished off the coast of Lewis. As I stood before the open grave of one of my companions whose body had been found... I wondered what strange providence had divided our ways." (M 20)

3. Conversion

He was converted at the age of twenty-two in a Greenock church. He describes the moment. "It was... as if Someone had opened the long-shut door of my heart and walked in... God, I felt, had in mercy broken through the awful barrier of my sin, and had saved me from its dominion, guilt and power... all things seemed to smile at this great wonder – a sinner reconciled to God." (M 22-23)

"I found that the experience of that evening was not a unique or isolated thing. It was not an emotional release or any upsurge of mere feeling [or] a passing phase of mental exaltation... Spiritual love, peace, joy, with the consciousness of God's presence in our lives, are aspects of Reality deeper and more solid than anything belonging to the world of mere nature." (M 24-25)

While a student, theism began to lose meaning for him, but he then regained it; he does not say how. Thereafter he never doubted, almost as if faith did not imply the possibility of doubt. (M 30)

The Diary mentions that its author was sometimes 'transported' beyond himself (as distinct from having out-of-body experiences). Yet joyful phases also give way to times of grief for sin, painful separation from the Beloved, and "the hand of the cruel" Satan. And there "is sometimes at the heart of Christian experience a deep inarticulate pain which may be beyond the ken of many Christian people and ministers". (M 85-86) Murdo does not elaborate, or identify this pain as sorrow, but his remark calls to mind the entry for December 13, 1962:

> In those days my mind and heart were not overburdened with the persistent sorrow which lodges there now. Many things contribute to this sorrow, such as the state of God's cause; the blanket of spiritual death which is over the visible Church; lack of Christian fellowship; and the daily warfare with 'the body of death'. (*Rom.* 7: 24)

He kept dreams in their place. Once "I dreamt I saw myself walking alone toward the green meadow near the Swainbost shore where... I used to play as a boy. In [a] group stood a Person whom I knew to be the Lord... He welcomed me into the company and most tenderly spoke to me, but what he said I may not tell. It was... a cherished word of love... I never had a dream since in which I saw the Lord Jesus... [But] if one were to leave the solid rock of Scripture for such night visions one would be very unwise." (M 26-27)

An outstanding tenor like his father, Murdo sang at Gaelic concerts; once converted he felt called to the ministry instead. He studied for University entry, graduated from Edinburgh University, and was ordained after three years at the Free Church College. He married Mary Fraser, from Strathpeffer; they had two daughters, Anne and Mary, and one surviving son, David, his editor today.

4. Ministry

After four years in the then considerable bilingual charge of Fort Augustus and Glenmoriston he transferred to Glasgow, where he developed the bilingual Partick Highland charge. He saw this congregation through the 1930s Depression and the Second World War, except for a stint as Gaelic Chaplain in Portsmouth and Plymouth. His health suffered and in 1951 he left for the rural parish of Resolis in the Black Isle, retiring in 1967.

With colleagues he was a reconciler, his year as Moderator noted for peace. Yet he was immovably courageous in his convictions, for example in the books and pamphlets he wrote. In private he was enraptured by God's intimate presence, dismal in His absence. These were not simply his interpretations of natural mood swings, just as 'spirituality' for instance does not simply mean 'little engaged with the material world'. He has been described as the most attractive and well-regarded preacher in the Highlands in his day. (John A. Morrison, *Am Pàipear* no. 339, Uist: June 2014) In the pulpit his language was orderly and poetic, his manner engaging and tender. His exegesis was kin to the English Puritans, his public prayer spontaneous and deeply spiritual. Every congregation in his Church and others in Britain and North America invited him to be their pastor.

He may be remembered for his writings but saw personal evangelism as his special work. On approaching retirement he developed cancer; his cherished, selfless wife cared for him, to the detriment of her health, until his death in 1974.

DC

David Campbell

Publications by the Revd Murdoch Campbell

Books

God's Unsettled Controversy (London, circa 1944)
Thy Own Soul Also or The Crisis in the Church (Glasgow 1945)
The King's Friend (Glasgow 1946)
The Coming Storm (Glasgow 1948)
Gleanings of Highland Harvest (1953)
The Diary of Jessie Thain (1955)
The Loveliest Story Ever Told (Inverness 1962)
In All Their Affliction (Inverness 1967)
Everlasting Love: Devotional Sermons (Edinburgh:
    Knox Press 1968)
From Grace to Glory: Meditations on the Book of
    Psalms (Banner of Truth Trust 1970)
No Night There: Devotional Sermons (Stornoway 1972)
Memories of a Wayfaring Man (Inverness 1974)
Tobraichean Solais: Wells of Joy (Covenanters Press 2013)

Dutch translations:
*Des Konings vriend : Het leven en sterven Norman
    Macdonald* (C. B. van Woerden Jr te Akkrum,
    Utrecht 1961)
Herinneringen van een Pelgrim (trs. J. Kooistra,
    Veenendaal 1978)

Dagboek van Jessie Thain (J. Kooistra 1980)
Nalezingen van de Highland-oogst (J. Kooistra,
    Gorinchem 1995)
In al hun benauwdheid: pastorale memoires van een
    Schotse predikant (trs. Ruth Pieterman: Gouda 2013)

Pamphlets

The Earth-bound Vision: A Critical Examination of
    Pre-millennialism
After Bishops – What? : The New Peril
Christians and the Use of Nuclear Weapons

Tract

When my Heart Smiled

Lightning Source UK Ltd.
Milton Keynes UK
UKOW05f1939281114

242365UK00003B/46/P